THE TIME IS AT HAND!
(New Edition)

Book 1 of *Chronicles at the End of the World* series

THE TIME IS AT HAND!

Scientific Predictions concerning the Future of America, ALL coming true Now!

(NEW EDITION)

By
Lt.Colonel T.L. Harlan (Ret.)
Former U.S. CounterIntelligence Agent

Patriots' Press
Pahrump, Nevada

PUBLISHED BY

Patriots' Press, Inc.

An imprint of the
St. John Chrysostom Publishing House
1970 N. Leslie Street, Box 553
Pahrump, NV 89060
http://patriotspress.myfreesites.net

ISBN-13: 978-0-9977585-3-5
(Paperback)

Library of Congress Catalog Number:
LCCN 2016900651

First Printing: August, 2015
Second Printing: December, 2015
Updated Edition: February, 2019

International Distribution Rights: Amazon Books.
Also available on Kindle.

PRINTED IN THE UNITED STATES OF AMERICA

PRELUDE TO DISASTER
(Original 2014 Preface)

· Is the United States and/or Israel going to be attacked again in the target year of 2018 by Muslim radicals, perhaps sometime around the anniversary of the September 11th Twin Towers Attack—possibly even more devastatingly this time—or will mitigation occur and that be held off until the next 17 Year Cycle conclusion in the year 2035, instead?

· Will one of the terrorist targets *this* cycle (any time after the 2017 Jewish High Holidays) be Las Vegas, Nevada, which is known to radicals as "Sin City"?

· Will the worst Wall Street Stock Market crash in the nation's history begin at some point after next year (after the Jewish High Holy Days of Rosh Hashanah and Sukkot of the Hebrew Calendar), which may then turn into a Great Recession lasting several years – or will this, too, be held off for one cycle, until the year 2035?

· What does the coming alignment of 4 Blood Moons, and the end of the Jewish Shemitah Year, portend for the 7 year period following September, 2015, when this harbinger in the sky will appear? Why are Christian churches across America beginning to go ballistic over this approaching prophetic "Sign in the heavens"?

• Will little Israel again have to defend itself from a military onslaught from the many massive Arab nations surrounding it, possibly beginning in 2018 (the Punishment Cycle Year) or shortly thereafter; or will a mitigation save us for another 17 years?

Whenever it does happen, will the U.S. then be drawn into a protracted war in the Middle East helping to defend the tiny Jewish State that Islamic extremists have vowed to "wipe off the face of the earth"?

• Will more American lives be lost in the year 2018 than at any other point in this national crisis (the Divine "punishment cycle" IAW Torah Law of the Bible), and will it be from attacks of Nature-gone-wild (as well as crazed home-grown terrorists), rather than from battle casualties overseas or from a resurgent Ebola Epidemic (or other such deadly disease), which experts are also predicting looms on the horizon?

• In the years that follow, is the Ark of the Covenant about to be discovered and the Jewish Temple rebuilt, after the destruction of the Dome of the Rock Mosque in Jerusalem; with the Vatican thereafter possibly being destroyed by fire by Muslim terrorists, thus shifting the "Time-Piece" of God's Plan for the Ages from Rome to Jerusalem?

• Is the killer earthquake known as "The Big One" on the West Coast of the USA going to occur at some point in *this* Locust Punishment Cycle year (2018), or the next (2035), destroying San Francisco and Hollywood? Will Seattle be included? Or will they all catch the next seismic cycles happening during the years 2035 and 2052, instead?

· Are the Hawaiian Islands then going to suffer massive damage from a devastating Tidal Wave from such a killer quake, or are they safe for another 17 years as well?

Are all these Time Tables confusing? "Are you sure this is scientific?" you ask. Don't worry, it will all be explained!

· Is the President of the United States whom we elect (or re-elect) in 2020 going to be assassinated or otherwise die while still in office, which sociologists are wary of?

The answer to some of these disturbing questions may very well be "yes," unfortunately, according to some leading experts in the fields of economics, seismology, sociology, and prophecy.

Are you one of those people who "don't believe in all that religious bunk"?

Well, you are not alone!

Many Actuary Analysts are not religious, either. But they still predict the future! (And most are frighteningly accurate, sorry to say). Dr. Alvin Toffler, an agnostic sociologist and Professor at Cornell University, likewise correctly predicted the future on many points in his books *Future Shock* and *The Third Wave*. Did you know even non-Christian hedonist Wall Street analysts and Stock Brokers now use computer programs that similarly "predict the future" of market trends, some possessing an amazingly high degree of accuracy?

In like manner, the predictions in this book are not based solely on Biblical Prophecy, worthy as that field of study may be, nor does the author claim any kind of "divine revelation" like some supermarket-tabloid occult Seer, or "psychic"; but instead we have used prognostication devices incorporating a panoply of factoid gathering from the Social Sciences, socio-economic trends, geological research, international political developments, World Religion forecasts, and the like.

Just as a matrix of Actuarial Tables, properly employed with the right medical data, can pinpoint right down to the very year a certain person will die, even 30 years in advance, so we can know – at least with some degree of certainty – the probable outcome of select world events.

This is a new and developing art, thanks largely to the rapid evolution of Computer Science. It is not infallible, but it *is* often accurate. You see the results of these complex geometric and/or algebraic matrices and computer algorithms based on Probability Theory every day, and don't even realize it. When you turn on the Weather Channel and watch "storm tracker radar," you are not actually seeing cloud-cover photographs from a satellite, as it appears to be, when you are viewing a "Future-cast," but rather a computer generated "probability model" of where the storm is headed next. It is not as simple as merely looking at which direction on the map the hurricane is currently heading then predicting it will go there. There are too many variables that could, and will, veer the storm onto another course.

The A.I. program developed by the U.S. National Weather Service and run on a Cray Computer, one of the largest in the world, can forecast as accurately as it does only because a huge amount of geological and meteorological and other atmospheric data is continuously fed into it real-time. Thus, it usually can pinpoint down to the exact hour, sometimes to the minute – county by county – where the rain will start falling, how fast the wind will be, if a tornado will touch down, etc.

Contrariwise to that, however, I do not claim everything will come to pass exactly as predicted in this book, (no human can know that), but merely that in accordance with Probability Theory much of it is *likely* to come to pass.

My college degree was in Political Science, and my experience was for many years working for the U.S. Government, both as a Federal Investigator (Special Agent) and as a Strategic Global Intelligence Officer. I originally wrote the notes for this book in the Summer of 1971, on a beach in Hawaii, when I discovered the amazing accuracy of the prognostication devices involved, originally written in the mid-20th Century by Dr. Gordon Lindsay and others, as explained in this book.

Since then, this "Presage Matrix" that foreshadows future events hit the nail on the head dozens of times, accurately predicting such things as the Moslem attack on the U.S. Marine Compound in Beirut in 1984, the attempt to assassinate President Ronald Reagan by the shooter John Hinckley, the Muslim air attack on the Pentagon in 2001, the attempt to assassinate President George Bush at the same time with a synchronized air strike on the White House (which brave American

Patriots aboard Flight 93 thwarted over an empty field in Pennsylvania), the U.S. Recession and Stock Market plunge of 2008, and now the national disasters predicted to hit our country in the year 2018 – unless mitigating factors forestall or lessen the suffering, as detailed herein.

Lt.Colonel T.L. Harlan (Ret.)
Former U.S. Intelligence Officer
Thanksgiving, 2014

PREFACE TO NEW EDITION
(*Updated 2019*)

For the reader new to Predictive Analysis, the subject matter of this book may at first seem overwhelming. But not to worry, this is not a textbook for understanding the subject, it is merely a collection of some "gems" we present to you in narrative form, much like a novel. Only, we are not dealing with fiction here...

Predictive Analytics is a new science, still being developed, encompassing a variety of statistical techniques from data mining, predictive modelling, and machine-learning, which then analyzes current and historical facts to make predictions about future or otherwise unknown events. For example, the Police Departments of several big cities have now started using a computer algorithm for this purpose, to predict *where* crimes will occur and *when*. Sound impossible? Guess what, it actually works!

The trouble is, when analyzing Big Picture global events, government and secular scientists eschew adding any religious data or prophecies from the Bible into their computer programs (even though 100% of them have come true in history so far), thus skewing the outcomes and making them far less accurate in their predictions. A truly *wise* scientist would not ignore religious realities, even if he was an atheist.

Now, let us look at specifics as to what has just occurred over the past five years, since this book was first published. This is an update for people who have already read it and understand how the Matrix works. If you have not, don't worry, simply understand THAT IT WORKS – as we are about to describe.

The 17 year cyclical "Punishment Year" for national sins, unfolding in the following historical stories you are about to read—originally written many years in advance of the events foretold—but applying only to Israel and America (for reasons explained later), was **2018**.

Now, follow me: The Orthodox Christian New Year for 2018 began on October 1, 2017, as reckoned by the Jerusalem Patriarchate of the Orthodox Catholic Church in the Holy Land. And New Year's Day, 2018, began a few days before that (at the end of September, 2017), as celebrated by Orthodox Jews in Israel using the Hebrew liturgical calendar. The Fiscal Year 2018 in America, as reckoned by the U.S. Government, likewise began on October 1, 2017. It is just how the calendar works.

On that exact day, the national punishments/ divine warnings began in the USA. The largest mass shooting in American history occurred on October 1st in Las Vegas, Nevada, (so-called "Sin City"), leaving over 800 victims wounded or injured and nearly 60 dead, **just as predicted in the First Edition of this book – years before it happened!**

Then, at the close of that same year, near the end of October, 2018, the largest mass shooting of Jews in American history occurred at the Tree of Life Synagogue in Pittsburgh, Pennsylvania, again putting the whole nation in mourning (both the USA and

Israel), to conclude that Punishment Cycle Year – again, *just as predicted!*

During the same time period in question, from near the end of 2017 through the end of 2018, as the Matrix prognosticated in advance, there were more than 100 massively destructive wildfires throughout the United States, particularly in the West. According to federal government statistics, this produced an actual total of over 100,000 out of control fires in the wild, destroying over 15 million acres, including the largest wildfire in the history of the State of California. Combined, they razed to the ground an estimated 50,000 homes and buildings – being **officially recorded as the worst "fire year" in more than a decade.**

Likewise, the predicted 17-Year–Cycle of *2018 went down in the record books as also being one of the worst years for destructive storms in some 20 years,* also detailed in the original edition of this book (which, by the way, was submitted for copyright to the Library of Congress in 2014).

The 2017-18 hyperactive catastrophic hurricane seasons featured a total of over 30 named storms, 18 hurricanes and 8 monster cyclones, with a total of $333.3 BILLION (U.S. Dollars) in damages, the costliest tropical cyclone seasons on record. Causing over 3,400 human deaths combined, the 2017-18 storms were the worst to pummel the United States in over a decade. Their destructiveness was an important part of the predicted 2018 Divine Discipline Year. And it came to pass just as foretold.

Other national catastrophes falling on us last year, further demonstrating the accuracy of the

Matrix, included a record number of mass shootings, school children murders, and cop killings. They were happening so frequently, most Americans lost sight of the fact that a total of **268 Mass Shootings occurred in the U.S. in 2018**, according to Congressional Reports at the Gun Violence Archive in Washington, D.C.

More school massacres happened that year than at any other time. More civilian Americans died from gun violence in the USA than military Service Members were killed by enemy combatants while serving overseas, making it more dangerous to live in the United States than to live in combat zones in the Middle East!

The mass deaths of children murdered at schools, especially, kept the nation in perpetual mourning throughout the 17-year cyclical Punishment Year of 2018.

THE RESULT OF ALL THIS IS THAT THE SCIENTIFIC PREDICTIVE ANALYSIS MECHANISM DETAILED IN THIS BOOK PROVED TO COME TRUE, ONCE AGAIN, IN 2018, JUST AS IT DID IN 2001, AND IN 1984, AND 1967, and so forth every 17 Years (mentioned in the Bible as a destructive locust cycle).

But there were also important mitigating events that tempered the 2018 Warning Year, as well. It could have been far worse. For example, in 1967 as mentioned above, during the national immorality of the Hippie Era, President Nixon was in power and it was the high point of the Vietnam War. We lost more American lives that year than at any other time during the war. Thousands of U.S. soldiers were slaughtered that year alone. But 17 years later, in 1984, President Reagan was in power and the nation was undergoing a moral revival. That Punishment Year we lost nearly 300 Marines in a Moslem Terrorist attack. A terrible thing, but a far lesser number of dead. That is because there were mitigating factors.

So, what softened the blow on how bad it **might** have been last year, allowing us to dodge the **worst** of the Divine National Judgements on the sins of modern America?

Now, lest this skew your understanding of the answer, here I must explain before you read what follows below that I personally did NOT vote for Mr. Trump when he first ran for President. So, this is NOT a comment on him personally, or how good or not good of a Christian or a politician he may or may not be. This is simply an explanation of the fact that when a nation's leaders—regardless of Political Party—enact righteous laws, the righteous of the land are blest thereby; and when said leaders legalize and legitimize sins, even law-abiding citizens will suffer from the consequences – *not just those indulging in the sins!* (cf., Matthew 5:45).

Thus, President Trump's decision to recognize Jerusalem as the Capital City of Israel in 2018 had far greater repercussions, around the world and in history, than most readers are aware of. ***This was a direct fulfillment of Biblical prophecy, the importance of which should not be underestimated!***

Both American Christians and Israeli Jews immediately recognized the U.S. President as being a "New King Cyrus," and flooded the airwaves with that important understanding of world affairs. King

Cyrus was a pagan, not a Jew, an Unbeliever not a Believer; yet he was nonetheless chosen by the God of Israel to fill that High Office – because in the very year prophesied in the Hebrew Bible, 70 years after the Babylonian Captivity began, Cyrus chose to obey the promptings of the Holy Spirit and signed the legal declaration allowing the Jews to return to the Holy Land and once again rebuild their Temple in Jerusalem.

To refresh the reader's memory, this is history from Old Testament times, when the I.D.F. (Israeli Defense Forces) were captured as Prisoners of War by the invading Iraqi Army of the Babylonian Empire, then allowed to return to their homeland 70 years later when the Persian Empire overthrew the Capital City of Babylon (near modern Baghdad), in exact and amazing fulfillment of Biblical prophecy given years in advance of the event that occurred.

Now, in modern times, the United States was the first—and so far only—country   to recognize Jerusalem as the capital of Israel. The United Nations condemned the U.S. for this action. NATO did not support it. Even our allies would not stand with us. NO OTHER COUNTRY ON EARTH STOOD WITH THE BIBLICAL NATION OF ISRAEL EXCEPT THE U.S.A. (That is an important point played out again and again in this book). President Trump bravely opened the U.S. Embassy in Jerusalem on May 14, 2018, **exactly 70 years to the day after the founding of the modern State of Israel!**

Many Christians and Jews see this as the very Hand of God working in human history.

This fulfilling of Bible Prophecy is of incredible importance to the Divine Timetable. And as national leaders make good choices, so all the people of the land will be blest accordingly. Thus, the Punishment Year of 2018 was highly mitigated, and not nearly as bad as it **could** have been, thanks to Donald Trump listening to his Jewish daughter and Christian White House Advisors.

There was also another mitigating factor that helped us out last year, which most Americans tend to also look passed, because they don't realize the importance of it – due to not seeing things the way the Almighty Judge of the World sees them...

One of the most grievous national sins for which the USA is under Divine Judgement is the horrifying mass murders of innocent preborn babies. The Bible says their "blood cries out from the ground to God" for justice. (Genesis 4:10). If this terrible sin were to again be made illegal, just as slavery was finally illegalized after a horrific national punishment, then the Divine "Hand of Judgement" would be stayed.

President Trump has a record of appointing Conservative judges who believe in traditional morality. In his first two years in office, he has nominated over 130 new Federal Judges, including two Justices of the United States Supreme Court. This is more than any of the past three Presidents were able to accomplish! For the **first** time in more than 40 years, since the Ultra-Liberal atheistic feminist Baby Killers came to power and had the Supreme Court legalize sodomy, adultery, and abortion, and **illegalize** Prayer in Schools, the moral majority of Americans—known as the "Silent Majority"— FINALLY have a chance to again have righteous laws enacted across the country, thus greatly mitigating Supernal disciplinary measures against us as a nation.

The third such mitigation factor that occurred, softening THIS 17-year-cycle judgment, likewise began in 2017 and ran through 2018, right on schedule, as predicted. As explained later in this book, when there is on-going national repentance of sins, there is an automatic staying of the hand of judgment for that particular punishment cycle. This next one might not seem that important to an outsider, at first, but through the eyes of a Celestial Judge it is quite important: The gross sexual immorality that began in Hollywood, then spread throughout our land, is finally coming to light... and being addressed.

Court legal actions against California movie moguls, and business leaders throughout the country, who have preyed on the weak of both sexes, is being exposed – *and punished*. Sexual exploitation of employees and the vulnerable is no longer being tolerated. This is actually a very important spiritual cleansing for our nation!

In like manner, the Roman Catholic Church in the USA, with its forced demand of celibacy for ALL Clergy, has proven to be a loophole for homosexual activists and MANBLA pedophiles to gain entrance into the ranks of ministers and teachers of private educational institutions and parishes, to wreak havoc among Catholic congregations. As the Vatican spokesman said, *some* of these sexual perverts were not even authentic priests, but had faked false paperwork just to gain access to the vulnerable for exploitation.

What the Ultra-Liberal mainstream News Media refuses to report, however, is that the vast majority of both Laity AND Clergy of the Church of Rome are **glad** to see this clean-up, long overdue, finally take place. 99% of Catholic Priests are good holy Men of God, who WARNED their Bishops of the few bad apples that should have been dismissed long ago, and are now glad to see that is finally being done – the cancer is being cut out of the Body!

This is an important catharsis taking place in our religious Houses of Worship throughout the country, effecting everyone, whether they are Catholic or not. On one hand, it is the Judgment of God being felt in 2018. But on the other hand, it is also part of a spiritual renewal movement that is helping prevent an even worse national judgment against us this "Locust Punishment Cycle."

THE JOINT EFFECT OF THESE MITIGATING FACTORS LESSENED THE JUDGMENT ON THE COUNTRY DURING THE 2018 DIVINE DISCIPLINE YEAR, EXACTLY AS THIS BOOK PREDICTED SEVERAL YEARS AGO WHEN FIRST PUBLISHED!

So, for instance, the coming national economic crash – which **could** have resulted in a deep Recession or even a Depression, which statistically should have begun no later than 2017 – has, thankfully, been forestalled... for a period of time. That is because we are NOT, as the secularist prognosticators would have you believe, dealing merely with cold scientific equations for predictive analysis, but we are dealing with the hand of the

Living God bringing these things about, **when and how He so chooses**, which the above mitigating factors have clearly influenced on our behalf.

The Bottom Line of all this is: *The future is liquid and ever-changing. We can change our own destinies!*

A final word to the reader. Please remember, this is not primarily Bible Prophecy. That is not the subject of this book, though we are wise enough to include religious data into the equation of Predictive Analysis. And it does not cover the whole world. Israel and the United States are the only nations on Earth that have this unique, if not bizarre, supernatural relationship.

Also, as you read further about these strange 17 Year Cycles, remember nothing says national disasters in Israel or America are *limited* to such years as 2001, 2018, 2035, 2052, etc. Top economists and financial experts warn a global financial collapse is indeed coming, at some point or another, and cannot be stopped... only forestalled or delayed. And it will be international, not just confined to America.

In like manner, geologists and other federal government scientists predict the devastating Pacific Coast super-quake, as described later in the narrative, is already overdue and could happen at **any time**. The same is true for the mega-faultline stretching from the Great Lakes to the Gulf of Mexico, which the Mississippi River runs along, and traditionally has divided the USA into East and West. However, if such "super-quakes" have not occurred in those areas by 2035, *I sure wouldn't want to be living there at that time!*

DEDICATION:

For Matushka Yolanda Cecilia (Harlan),
My inspiration and my joy!

The Book of Revelation, Chapter 22, Verse 10:

And the Angel saith unto me, *Seal not up the sayings of the prophecies of this book, for as to their fulfillment…*

T.L. Harlan

The Time is at Hand!

"The wise man watches the road ahead, and sees danger approaching in the distance, and takes appropriate action. He is able to hide himself in safety in time. But the fool ignores where he is going, and thus travels to his destruction."

-- Book of Proverbs, chapter 27, verse 12
(Eastern Orthodox Septuagint Bible)

CHAPTER 1

The Long Hot Summer

Little Timmy Carpenter, all of nine years of age, stood motionless at the mouth of the darkened alley. He nervously peered into the moving shadows at the far end before stepping from the safety of the populated, sunlit street. Gulping, he cautiously edged his way into the shadowy world of the back alley of the Big City. His Mom, one of the staunch faithful at the Black Baptist church down the street, had *warned* him about taking short-cuts on the way to the market when he ran errands for her, so his conscience bothered him a little.

He bristled and his pace quickened as a stray cat over-turned an empty garbage can it had leaped from with a yowl, as he walked by in the semi-darkness. Months' worth of uncollected trash and human refuse were littered everywhere across the walk. The stench of the urine-soaked alley was familiar, yet sickening nonetheless.

He passed by the back door of one squalid, single-room tenement with the screen door propped open in the hot evening air. He could hear the yelling of an angry man inside knocking around a shrieking woman.

Not to worry, he told himself nervously. A pimp

was just lecturing one of his girls. That's all.

He was nearing the end of the alley now. He had successfully run the gauntlet. Beginning to relax, his pace slackened... just a bit.

Then, suddenly, out of the shadows came a deep, low voice. A skinny middle-aged Hispanic man was sitting on some filthy cement steps with a brown paper sack in one hand.

"Hey, kid. Come here!" the voice ordered. But Timmy kept going, stiffening his pace.

"Got any change?" the voice called after him.

"Just a wino," he told himself. "No problem."

Timmy kept walking.

Other than that, the alley was deserted. Not a soul in sight. Then, from out of nowhere, a large newspaper page caught in the hot late-afternoon wind tumbled by in near silence. There was a hint of rain in the air.

Timmy casually grabbed at the passing paper, and just by luck hooked it. He looked at the front page and thoughtfully slowed to a halt. The only sounds in the stillness were a distant dog barking and a police car siren barely audible from the other side of the city. In the dim and fading light he read the headlines.

There was a picture of the earth, or a globe, that was cracked down the middle and splitting apart. Beneath this, but taking up nearly the whole page, it said in bold black letters simply, "CHRIST IS THE ANSWER."

A gust of hot summer wind caught the newspaper and blew it out of Timmy's hands, where it carried on its endless tumbling journey down the back allies and mean streets of the Big City at dusk, until it was totally obscured from view by the deepening twilight falling all around.

The darkness of night was rapidly approaching.

"If ye be willing and obedient ye shall eat the good of the land, but if ye rebel and refuse, ye shall be devoured by the sword."

— Isaiah 1:19-20

CHAPTER 2

The Founding of a Continent

Springtime, 1485. Genoa, Italy.

"'Admiral Christopher Columbus, Viceroy and Governor,' that is what I saw when I was in prayer, Bart. I started making some notes for a book I am going to write someday. I want to call it, *The Book of Prophecies* by Christopher Columbus. But how will any of these things come true if we cannot even get funding to make an exploratory voyage? Some 'Admiral' I am, I don't even own a ship!"

"Peace, my brother," said Bart. "You must not give up your dream, even with this bad news."

"It is not just you returning from England empty-handed, Bartholomew, getting turned down by King Henry. I, also, went to the High Court of Portugal, to see King John, and explain to him how financially lucrative it would be for him if I could sail his Royal Flagship to discover the New World."

"Well, what did he say, Chris?"

"He threw me out on my ear."

"Perhaps we will have to go to Rome and see the Pope himself, to explain how important this is," suggested his brother.

Seven years later, Christopher and Bartholomew Columbus were on the seaside docks of the Italian Riviera, outfitting ships for a long sail.

"I am glad you did not give up on your dream, Chris. Thank God King Ferdinand and Queen Isabella of Spain finally funded your upcoming voyage, or we would be stuck," said Bart.

"They didn't do as much as you think," the other answered. "No real money. They let me eat for free in any Spanish territory, nothing more. And they pressed into service these three barely seaworthy merchant ships, so I could at least fly under their flag. But the sailors are not getting paid by the Crown, so the owners and crews of these vessels are not at all happy. I actually fear mutiny is a possibility once we reach the High Seas.

"No, Bart, the real reason we are able to make this voyage is because of our Jewish friends. They seem to be the only ones who really want us to find the New World."

"Well, of course! They need a place to escape to in order to avoid this wave of persecution that has started from the Spanish Inquisition," his brother said.

"And I hope to give them that," answered Columbus. "The Jewish banker Gabriel Sanchez, and his wealthy financier, Luis de SantAngel, and their Rabbi Isaac Abravanel, are the ones who are actually making this voyage possible – and God bless them for it!"

Admiral Columbus took leave of his brother on the dock and boarded the first of the three little ships, the *Saint Mary*. "Named after the Mother of Christ," he said, patting the oaken boards wet with seawater. "How appropriate. The Blessed Virgin shall become the Patron Saint of the New World. For the first land we come to I am going to name after the Holy Savior, or in Spanish (to keep the King and Queen happy), *San Salvador*."

Christopher Columbus walked onto the Bridge, nodded to the pilot at the wheel busy adjusting the compass, read the Ship's Log, then went to his State Room. There, he made some entries into his private diary.

He wrote: "Many have ridiculed me for attempting such a fool-hardy adventure. They think I am just a profiteer going on some risky expedition. Little do they realize I have been led by the Holy Spirit Himself, for something much greater than merely finding a trade-route to the Far East so European royalty can feast on Oriental spices! I am being blessed by Almighty God for a more important destiny. The hand of the Lord is indeed guiding me."

His thoughts were interrupted by a knock at the cabin door.

It was the First Mate. "Captain," the old Sea Dog said gruffly, "There be a gang of Jews on the dock wantin' to talk with ye."

Curious, Columbus walked off the deck and down the gangplank. But all he found was a frightened little Jewish family huddled together: A Spanish father, mother, and young daughter. "Sir, could we speak with you in private?" the father asked.

Columbus led them a few paces away from the dock workers. "Admiral, at our synagogue the Rabbi told us we should talk with you personally," the man said confidentially. "We want to go with you."

"This isn't a pleasure cruise we are going on, you know," answered Columbus. "It will be quite dangerous."

"We know. But we want to go anyway, even if it means risking our lives. We are willing to join the crew and work. Anything for a new start in life!"

"My husband suffered gruesome physical torture at the hands of the Spanish Inquisition," the young mother explained. "They were trying to get him to convert and leave the ancient Faith of Judaism."

At this, their little daughter, too young to know any better, handed Columbus the three yellow patches of cloth, the Star of David, they had all been forced to wear on their clothing but had recently removed, which was against the law. The Viceroy and Governor of the New World, flying under the flag of Spain, looked at the crumpled pieces of cloth in his hand, trying to decide what to do.

He looked around to make sure no one was watching, wadded them up, then threw them into the sea.

"You won't be needing these where **you** are going," he said.

"Welcome aboard."

"The hand of our God is upon all them, for good, who seek Him; but His power and His wrath are against all who forsake Him."

-- Ezra 8:22

CHAPTER 3

The Founding of One Nation under God

The Long Hard Winter of 1777. Valley Forge, Pennsylvania.

General George Washington, Supreme Commander of the Continental Army, sat in his Field Headquarters tent deep in thought. Famous for being a believing Christian and a Man of Prayer, he was praying now like he had never prayed before. Enemy forces lay on all sides. He was critically low on rations and on soldiers. Congress was not funding him properly. Restocking of ammunition and supplies was blockaded by enemy lines.

The whole Army, what was left of it, had to leave the battle ground and retreat to Valley Forge to spend the winter. It was America's darkest hour. It did not look like the 13 Colonies were going to win their Revolutionary War for Independence. The Stars and Stripes may never fly over this land again.

They would have already been done in if it had not been for the bravery and self-sacrifice of one man: Haym Salomon. A mild-mannered Jewish banker in New York City by day, and a Patriot Intelligence Officer of great skill by night. He had been arrested by the British, found guilty of being an American spy, and sentenced to death. But he cleverly managed to escape. When General Washington asked it of him, he had given his family fortune to help support the Continental Army. When that gave out, he went fund-raising among wealthy Jewish merchants from Europe, garnering the modern equivalent of nearly nine billion dollars for the War Effort!

George Washington could not thank him enough. He wrote in his diary, "May Mr. Salomon and the Jewish people living in America always be remembered for how they helped build this nation!"

The General locked himself into his private quarters and gave orders to the guard at the tent door that he did not wish to be disturbed. There, alone, he prayed for America... And wept.

"Lord, is this all for naught?" he entreated. "Am I just getting a lot of good men killed for no reason? Will we succeed in this fight? Will the 13 States unite and become one nation under God?"

Several hours passed.

Finally, Washington burst out of the door at full stride and called energetically for his private secretary.

A minute later, Anthony Sherman scampered to the General's HQ tent, quill-pen and parchment in hand.

"Close the door, Mr. Sherman," the Commander-in-Chief ordered. "Take a seat there at the table, and turn up the lamplight."

Pacing back and forth (for he could think better on his feet), Washington said, "Let me tell you what happened this very afternoon, and you take a memo.

"I was visited by an angel."

Sherman sat motionless, his pen suspended in the

air, as he stared at the Founder of Our Country.

"Just write it down!" ordered the General.

"Now, I do not know whether it was owing to the anxiety of my mind, or what, but this afternoon, as I was sitting at this very table engaged in preparing a dispatch, something in my compartment caught my attention. Looking up, I beheld standing opposite me a singularly beautiful being. So astonished was I, for I had given strict orders not to be disturbed, that it was some moments before I found my tongue to inquire the cause of the visit. A second, a third, and even a fourth time did I repeat the question, but received no answer from my mysterious visitor except a slight raising of the eyes toward Heaven.

"By this time I felt strange sensations spreading over me. I would have risen, but the riveted gaze of the being before me rendered volition impossible. I tried once more to speak but my tongue had become useless, as if paralyzed. All I could do was gaze steadily, vacantly, at my unknown visitor.

"Gradually the surrounding atmosphere grew luminous and the angelic spirit before me became more distinct to my eyes. I was only conscious of gazing fixedly at my unearthly companion.

"Presently I heard a voice saying, 'Son of the Republic, look and learn,' while at the same time my visitor extended an arm eastward.

"Now, I beheld a heavy white vapor at some distance rising fold upon fold. This gradually dissipated, and I looked upon a strange scene. Before me lay, spread out in one vast plain, all the continents of the world – Europe, Asia, Africa, and the Americas. I saw rolling and tossing between Europe and America the billows of the Atlantic Ocean. In this futuristic vision, I saw our country spreading out all the way to the Pacific Ocean, across which was Asia. 'Son of the Republic,' said the mysterious voice as before, 'Look and learn.'

"At that moment I beheld a dark shadowy being, but also like an angel, standing (or rather, floating in mid-air) between Europe and America. Dipping water out of the ocean in the hollow of each hand, he sprinkled some upon America with his right hand, while with his left he cast some over Europe. Immediately a cloud arose from these countries and joined in mid-ocean. For a while it seemed stationary, and then it moved slowly westward until it enveloped America in its murky folds. Sharp flashes of lightning gleamed through it at intervals, and I heard the smothered groans and cries of the American people."

[*Editorial Note:* England and elements of France in Europe, and the 13 States in America, all engaged in battle in the Revolutionary War, which was fought mostly on our shores here.]

"A second time the dark spirit dipped from the ocean and sprinkled it out as before. The heavy gray cloud was then drawn back into the ocean in whose heaving billows it sank as before.

"A third time I heard the mysterious voice saying, 'Son of the Republic, look and learn.' I cast my eyes upon America and beheld villages and towns and cities springing up one after another until the whole land from the Atlantic to the Pacific was dotted with them. Again I heard the mysterious voice saying, 'Son of the Republic, the end of a "century" of years approaches; look and learn.'

"And this time the dark shadowy angel turned his face to the South. From Africa I saw an ill-omened specter approach our land. It flitted slowly and heavily over every town and city in America. And I saw our citizens presently set themselves in battle array against one another, American soldiers fighting against their fellow Americans.

"But as I continued watching this panorama unfold, I saw a bright angel on whose brow rested a Crown of Light on which was imprinted the word 'Union.' He was bearing the American flag. He placed the flag between the divided nation and shouted, 'Remember, ye are Brethren!'

"Instantly, the American soldiers, casting down their weapons, became friends once more and united around the National Standard."

[*Editorial Note:* This indeed was an amazing look into the future granted to the Founder of Our Country wherein he was shown the coming Civil War, fought just as predicted nearly a hundred years after the Revolution. Note also the real issue that was being fought over was the sin of slavery, and freeing African-Americans, and not the secondary issue of "States' Rights" as the Confederacy contended.]

"Again I heard the mysterious voice saying, 'Son of the Republic, look and learn.' At this, the dark shadowy angel placed a trumpet to his mouth and blew three distinct blasts. Then, taking water from the ocean, he sprinkled it upon Europe, Asia, and Africa.

"Then my eyes beheld a fearful scene. From each of these continents arose thick black clouds that were soon joined into one. And through this mass there gleamed a dark Red light by which I saw hordes of armed men. These combined armies, moving with the cloud, marched by land and sailed by sea to America, which country was enveloped in the volume of that deadly dark cloud. And I dimly saw the vast armies devastate the whole country, from coast to coast, burning to the ground [at the same time] all those towns and cities which I had seen springing up before."

[*Editorial Note:* There is no way this kind of warfare could exist, or even been imagined, in Washington's day. World War III pictured here clearly will go thermonuclear from a surprise attack of the Reds against the USA: Communist China and her Asian allies, Eastern European Slavic countries of the former Soviet Union, and when this occurs in the future, some of the Muslim north African nations will have become more developed and be a modern atomic superpower as well. They will all be united in a type of Warsaw-Pact coalition against the United States and her allies.]

"As my ears listened to the thundering of the cannons, clashing of swords, firing of rifles, and the shouts and cries of millions in mortal combat, I again heard the mysterious voice saying, 'Son of the Republic, look and learn.' When this voice had ceased, the dark shadowy angel placed his trumpet once more to his mouth and blew a long and fearful blast.

"Instantly, an incredibly bright light of what looked like a thousand suns shone down from the sky above me and pierced and broke into fragments the dark cloud which enveloped America. At the same moment, the angel upon whose head still shone the word 'Union' and who bore our national flag in one hand and a sword in the other, descended from the heavens attended by legions of white spirits. These immediately joined the inhabitants of America, who I perceived were well-nigh overcome but who immediately, taking courage again, closed up their broken ranks and renewed the battle."

[*Editorial Note:* Two important points the reader should note. First, President Washington sees millions (plural) of Americans engaged in combat. That was an impossibility to foresee in his day, as the total population of the original 13 States was only a few thousand. Secondly, notice how the U.S. Armed Forces of the future has a national nuclear defense strategy. Though enough atomic warheads get through to burn down all our major cities at once, due to a surprise attack, further enemy ICBM missiles do not make it through – to entirely obliterate our nation – thanks to high-altitude nuclear interceptor rockets, the ONLY way to make sure you wipe out an entire fleet of hundreds of incoming ICBMs. (Which can be done even today in 2014 from sub-launched belligerents in both oceans surrounding the USA). So this futuristic scenario of warfare against our country is not at all far-fetched.]

"Again, amidst the fearful noise of the conflict I heard the mysterious voice saying, 'Son of the Republic, look and learn.' As the voice ceased, the shadowy angel for the last time dipped water from the ocean and sprinkled it upon the land. Instantly the dark cloud rolled back, together with the armies it had brought, leaving the citizens of America finally victorious!

"After that, once more I beheld the villages, towns, and cities springing up across the land where I had seen them before, while the bright angel, planting the Stars and Stripes he was carrying in the middle of the nation, cried out with a loud voice, 'While the stars remain, and the heavens send down dew upon the earth, so long shall the Union last.' And taking from his brow the crown on which was emblazoned the word, 'Union,' he placed it upon the American flag. All the people knelt down before the Lord and answered, 'Amen'!"

[*Editorial Note:* Notice that after this final national calamity, the American people are finally able to have spiritual revival and pray publicly (without being told it is against the law). Note also that due to the nuclear devastation of the Eastern Seaboard, our current National Command Authority, the capital of the United States will need to be moved to the Midwest – our "Heartland." In the future, Dallas, Texas or Tulsa, Oklahoma may be in line for becoming the new District of Columbia.]

"As I watched, this scene began to fade and dissolve. I at last saw nothing but the rising, curling vapor I had first beheld.

"This also finally disappeared, and I found myself once more gazing upon the mysterious visitor in my tent who, in the same voice I had heard before, said, 'Son of the Republic, what you have seen is thus interpreted: Three great perils will come upon your nation. The most fearful for her is the third. But the whole world united shall not prevail against her. Let every Son and Daughter of the Republic learn to live for God, their country, and Union!'

"With these words the vision vanished, and I started from my seat, the very one you are sitting at now, Mr. Sherman. And I felt I had been shown a prophetic vision wherein I had seen the birth, the progress, and the destiny of these United States of America."

"Lord, teach us how to number the days, so that we may apply our minds unto Wisdom."

— Psalms 90:12

CHAPTER 4

The Plague of Locusts: 17 Year Attack Cycle

Summer, 1941. Dallas, Texas.

Dr. Gordon Lindsay sat at his desk, working feverishly. The classroom was empty.

A Graduate Student walked in and inquired politely, "Professor? Is everything alright? You have been working in here all night, non-stop."

"Eureka!" He cried. "I found it! I've discovered the Secret Key! It was buried in the text all along. Look... Look here, Mr. Watson." He pointed toward a pile of charts and graphs on his desk, rummaging through them until he found the one he wanted.

"The reason no one has seen this before the 20th Century is because of some slight errors in Biblical Chronology made by earlier exegetes. They were filling in the gaps in their knowledge base with secular history dates. They were all so close – Archbishop Ussher of Ireland, Cyrus Scofield in his Reference Bible, the Venerable Bede, Bishop Eusebius in his *Church History* – but they all made the same mistake. Each one was just slightly off. And that is what led to all those false religious cults like Jehovah's Witnesses and Mormons and Christian Science getting their dates wrong, thus making their predictions way off.

"It is not that the Bible Prophecies are wrong, it is merely that our dates in the Gregorian Calendar were wrong!

"And that means, at some point in this very decade, before the year 1950 A.D., the Jewish People will be gathered up from around the world and go back to the Holy Land. The nation of Israel will be reborn in just the next few years! I know none of the churches are going to believe it, but I have to tell them anyway.

"O my God, Watson! Do you know what this means? This is the key to accurately predicting future events! Help me gather up all my notes and send them to the publisher. These findings must be put into print at once. "

"What should I call the manuscript?" he asked.

"Entitle the book, *God's Plan for the Ages*.

"But first, I'll have to write the White House. I must let President Roosevelt know his life is in danger!"

****

Summer, 1963. Washington, D.C.

Reverend Lindsay paced outside the White House front door. Why wouldn't they let him in? He had an appointment with the President's secretary, after all. But they kept him waiting for nearly an hour in a little side office, the sign on the door of which read simply, "Secret Service Detail."

Finally, the Supervisor of the Special Agents who had initially questioned him on why he wanted to see the Chief Executive arrived, and showed him in to an inner office.

"Now, Mr. Lindsay, how can we help you?" he said officiously.

"I don't expect you guys to understand all this. But if I could just speak with President Kennedy's secretary, and explain everything to her... I just want to make sure he is aware... Look, 20 years ago I tried to warn President Roosevelt of this same danger. But the White House ignored me then, too. And a few months later we were having the State Funeral for F.D.R."

"I can assure you, Mr. Lindsay, we take any threats against the Oval Office seriously. And we appreciate the citizenry alerting us to anything they have heard on the street. Go ahead and explain it to me, and I will make a report and be sure the President is briefed about it."

"Very well then," he began, "I'm Dr. Gordon Lindsay, Professor of Biblical Studies, from Dallas, Texas, and I have discovered a key to interpreting prophecies..."

Here, the U.S. Secret Service supervisor stopped writing, put down his pen, and peered over the rim of his reading glasses at the aged Minister.

"Look, I won't try to explain it all, let me just 'cut to the chase' and tell you it is a fact that William Henry Harrison was elected President of the United States in 1840. Then, just a few months later, in the Winter of 1841, he was dead."

"Yes," said the Special Agent, I remember my American History. But he wasn't assassinated, he simply died from pneumonia a few weeks after Inauguration Day in the snow."

"Right. But nevertheless, he died while in office. Let me continue.

"Exactly 20 years later, Abraham Lincoln was elected President in 1860. Then, the year after he was re-elected, in 1865, he fell to the assassin's bullet.

"Now, exactly 20 years after *that*, James A. Garfield was elected to the Presidency in 1880. And he, also, was assassinated a year later, in 1881."

"Yes, it is rather a strange coincidence, I agree," dismissed the supervisor as he wrote something on his pad of paper.

"Well, watch; this goes well beyond coincidence... Twenty years later, in 1900, William McKinley was President. Then, in 1901, he likewise was assassinated."

"But McKinley was elected in 1896," the Special Agent corrected him.

"True. However, he was re-elected in 1900. That's the key." The professor went on, "And it continues: In 1920, Warren G. Harding was elected President. Before his first term was over, he died in 1923."

"He wasn't assassinated," said the Secret Service man matter-of-factly."

"No, he died of pneumonia, like his predecessor. But he died while still in office nonetheless. That is the point.

"So, likewise, Franklin Delano Roosevelt, elected in 1940, exactly 20 years later. It didn't matter that he had served as President the term before that date, nor that he was re-elected after that date and didn't die until 1945. And it didn't matter that he died from a stroke rather than from an assassin. The thing is, he was elected in 1940 and died while serving in the Office of President of the United States!"

"And why is this, do you think, Mr. Lindsay?" the agent asked dryly.

"Well, it has to do with our National Punishment Cycles – due to our joint sins as a society."

The other man rolled his eyes. "So, now you think President Kennedy is in danger, just because he was elected in 1960, twenty years to the day later?"

"Well, yes... because he doesn't have any spiritual protection to defend himself from the curse."

"What is *that* supposed to mean?" the Special Agent arched his eyebrows.

"Well, you see, the Chief Executives of the nation who have succumbed to this 20-year malediction have all been rather, well, shall we say, not always living a committed Christian lifestyle?

"I mean, look at Warren Harding. His Administration was plagued with accusations from Congress of unethical behavior, and his list of mistresses visiting the White House was the Talk of the Town in his day.

"Same with F.D.R. He was quite the Lady's Man, and it was no secret, even outside of Washington, D.C.

"James Garfield came from a non-religious family so opposed to the Christian Revival going on when he was a boy, his father pulled him out of school just so he wouldn't have a Conversion experience.

"And Abraham Lincoln did not become a Christian until just a few days before he was assassinated. In fact, he had made arrangements with his wife's Pastor on Palm Sunday to make a public Profession of Faith in church the next weekend, on

Easter Sunday, when he was murdered like Christ on Good Friday."

"And so now, with J.F.K., Marylyn Monroe and a long line of mistresses are waiting on the sidelines for him, as well."

"Now, see here, Mr. Lindsay!" bristled the Special Agent in Charge. "You are talking about the sitting President of the United States!"

"Sorry, I didn't mean to offend. But you see, *if* the man in Office at the time of these special dates is living a truly Christian lifestyle, my study of the National Punishment historical cycles shows that he can deflect the curse and skip a cycle – that he won't be killed, even though the Devil sends evil people or diseases to attempt it.

"So, in other words, whoever is elected President in 1980, and in 2000, if they are Born-Again Christians and ask the nation for prayers on their behalf, they can annul the effects of any such assassination attempts. But then, whoever is elected in the year 2020, (or even in 2016 if he is re-elected for a second term), if that person has unethical practices, or lives a wild lifestyle, or gives the protection of the Chief Executive's Office to notorious public sinners, then the curse will resume, and that President will once again die before his or her term is up."

[*Editorial Note:* It is not only amazing that this formula repeated itself 7 times over the past couple hundred years of American history regarding the deaths of 7 Presidents, but the last two who did not die at their appointed 20 year interval – Ronald Reagan in 1980 and George Bush in 2000 – were both well known to be active and sincere Born Again Christians who believed in Biblical morality, and voted on laws accordingly.

Nevertheless, the assassinations were attempted. A deranged madman, John Hinckley, shot President Reagan in 1981, but brave Law Enforcement Officers took the rest of the bullets for him, thus saving his life. And terrorist mastermind Osama Bin Laden ordered the assassination of President Bush by sending an airliner full of innocent civilians to be a missile to crash into the White House in 2001.

But Sunday School teacher Todd Beamer, Tom Burnett, Jeremy Glick, Mark Bingham, and a handful of brave American patriots aboard United Airlines Flight 93 decided that if they were going to die that day, then they wanted their lives to count for something. So, they voluntarily gave up their lives by crashing the jet into an uninhabited field in Pennsylvania before it could reach its intended target and kill the President of the United States. (Because that is the caliber of heroes the USA produces).

However, it is possible this same Divine protection may not necessarily be afforded to whoever is elected in the years 2020 and 2040.]

The Special Agent in Charge said curtly, "Yes, well, I'll be sure to lecture President Kennedy on how he needs to be more religious. Thank you for your time, Mr. Lindsay." He stood up in a dimissory manner.

A few minutes later, after their guest had departed, the supervisor walked into the Secret Service Ready Room. "Who was that, Boss?" asked the agent seated at the typewriter.

"Oh, just some crazy Street Preacher," he said

nonchalantly, throwing his notes down on the desk in front of the agent.

"You want me to type up a report on it?"

"Hardly seems worth our while," the supervisor said, pouring fresh coffee. "You can probably just 'Round File' it."

****

24 November 1963. Dallas, Texas.

"Do you want me to put out an Arrest Warrant on this Gordon Lindsay character, Chief?" the Dallas Police Detective asked.

"No, the Secret Service just wants to question him. See if he'll come in voluntarily. He's supposed to be some kind of Dean of a Bible College around here. We just have to do a general sweep of 'All the Usual Suspects' within 72 hours of the Kennedy tragedy, to help the Feds out. The Governor called the Mayor last night at home and chewed his butt out really bad, I heard."

A few hours later Professor Lindsay was seated at a small wooden desk on a hard chair in an un-airconditioned bare room marked "Dallas Police Department Detective Squad." A hot, bright lamplight was placed in front of him. "Wow. Just like in the movies," he said under his breath.

"What was that?" the burly Police Sergeant snarled. "I wouldn't joke around if I were you, Mister. You are already in enough trouble."

"Why? What have I done?" the Minister asked.

At that moment a young Texas State Trooper walked briskly down the hall escorting his V.I.P. guest. He threw open the door to the Interrogation Room, announcing to the Dallas P.D. Sergeant, "This is Special Agent Irving from the U.S. Secret Service."

The Federal Investigator officiously swept into the room without greeting anyone or even looking up at the suspect. He motioned for the Police Officer to vacate his seat, whereupon he sat down and threw open his briefcase, pulling out a file.

"I don't have a lot of time," he said. "Let's just get straight to business. It will go a lot easier on you if you simply confess."

"Confess to what?" asked Dr. Lindsay.

"Don't get smart with me, boy!" he said to the older man. "What is your connection with the assassination of President Kennedy? How well did you know Lee Harvey Oswald? Were you his handler? Are you now or were you ever a member of the Communist Party?"

"I'm a Conservative Republican!" retorted the Minister, offended. "And I never even met Lee Harvey Oswald."

"That is very difficult to believe, Mr. Lindsay," barked the Secret Service man. "The hit on the President was put out in *your* city, the shooter Oswald lived right near *your* neighborhood, *your* son was already at the hospital after Kennedy's ambulance came in but before Secret Service Agents arrived, claiming he wanted to give blood to help out. And *you* were caught making threats against the President of the United States just a few months before this happened! That's too many coincidences for me,

Buster," he roared. "Now, *confess!*"

"What do you mean I was 'caught,' and was 'making threats'? I *voluntarily* reported to you guys my findings, begging you to alert the President and warn him of the danger. But you wouldn't do it because you were asleep at the wheel!"

"Now see here!" bellowed the Special Agent, not used to being treated like that. "We are going to lock you up and throw away the key if you don't talk!"

"I'm most happy to talk," answered the college professor. "That is how I make my living. I'll tell you about anything you want to know... if it is on a subject I know something about."

The Federal Investigator queried, "Then how did you know in advance that President Kennedy was going to be shot if you didn't have anything to do with it? You'll have to admit, that is pretty suspicious."

"The same way I knew President Roosevelt was going to die in office in 1945, and that Israel was going to be reborn as a nation in 1948, and much more!" answered the older man.

"Are you some kind of prophet or something?"

"No. But I **can** see into the future – at least a little bit."

"Does God tell you this stuff?" the Fed asked, wondering if the suspect might be psychologically unhinged.

"No. Not directly. Not like you are thinking. Not like some occult 'seer' looking into a crystal ball...

"But He did show me the key of how to decipher certain world events – to know **some** things that are going to happen in the future."

"Yeah? Like what?"

"Well, for instance, I can tell you that the current 'Police Action' in Vietnam is going to burgeon into a full-fledged war, so that in a few years from now, by 1967, we will be at the height of the crisis, losing thousands of American boys over there. And that in the same year Israel will be invaded by its Islamic Arab neighbors and also have to go to war."

"How do you know all that?" the Investigator asked, growing interested but still suspicious. "Are you in contact with Foreign Intelligence Operatives?"

"Well, if you really want to know, let me show you..." Dr. Lindsay pulled a used paperback copy of his book *God's Plan for the Ages* out of his jacket pocket and began flipping through the worn pages, looking for various charts and graphs to show him.

"You see, our nation is tied in with the State of Israel. What happens to them, happens to us."

"Why is that?" the G-Man asked, his tone softening a bit.

"Well, in times past, most Christians thought it was because that since the U.S.A. was founded as a Christian nation, different among all other countries on earth, we had somehow replaced the Jewish nation – we were the New Israel, so to speak. That was called 'Replacement Theology.' But nowadays that theory is no longer popular.

"Since the good Lord has made it clear He has now forgiven the Jews for rejecting their Messiah, after their Holocaust Offering in the Nazi Death Camps, and proclaimed the 2,000 year old Diaspora of the Jewish People is over, most Christians—both Protestants and Catholics—now believe the Jews' ancient Covenant with the Almighty is still intact, and it will in fact be the actual physical nation of Israel that fulfills Bible Prophecies concerning their future.

"So, the other popular theory of why America is a specially chosen nation, then, working in tandem with the State of Israel, which is now gaining more acceptance, is because of the fact that no other nation on earth has a larger Jewish population than the United States. We have more Jews living here than even in Israel itself! And we have always been a safe-haven for the persecuted Jews, from our founding. Thus, we enjoy the same privileges – and duties and responsibilities – as they do.

"Now, that being the case, look at American History..."

He held the open book out for Agent Irving, who was now truly interested. Pointing to one of the graphic aids, the aged Bible Professor continued, "Around 1729 the 13 original Colonies were forming and George Washington was about to be born. 17 years after that birth of our fledgling country, the American people were disciplined by our having to fight in 'King George's War' in 1746."

"Why 17 years?" asked the Federal Agent. "What is so special about *that?*"

"Well, it is one of God's unique numbers that keeps reappearing throughout the Bible. Ancient Israel was punished with war or some other national calamity every 17 years, to make the people repent when they had gone astray. However, if they were in the midst of a spiritual revival at the time, the Divine Retribution would skip a cycle.

"Notice also how the Creator put into His creation the locust, which hibernates for 17 years, then they all come back to life at once, sweeping across the land and causing devastation from the destruction of crops of food so blighted.

"So, now, 17 years from King George's War brings us to 1763. And what happened then? The French and Indian War. It was the last year of it, but the point is, hundreds more American lives were lost in warfare at that time. Another 'national punishment,' so to speak.

"Okay, 17 years later, right on schedule, our country again suffers much loss by fighting the Revolutionary War with Britain. (1780 is right in the middle of the war, which lasted from 1775 to 1783). A lot of Americans killed, almost destroying our new nation. Terrible tragedy.

"But, the U.S.A. recovers and grows.

"Now, interestingly, when 17 years rolls around again, we are in the middle of the Second Great Awakening, a religious revival across the country. People are repenting of their sins already, so they don't *need* to be disciplined by the chastising hand of the Heavenly Father. Thus, in 1797 the only warfare that plagued our country was a short Naval War with France – just a few battles at sea. *The Punishment Cycle was mitigated!* That is an important principle.

"Now, another 17 years passes by and it brings us to 1814, right in the middle of the 'War of 1812,' which did not end until 1815. So, these dates do not indicate when a war is going to begin, but its high point, or when we are losing the most American lives. And as you will see, it does not always indicate warfare: *Any* wide-scale national disaster serves the purpose, so to speak.

"So, 17 years later brings us to 1831. The Nullification Act occurs and the country prepares to go to war yet again. This time a Civil War. But wait!

That is also the time period when both the Revival Movement of Charles Finney and the anti-slavery Abolitionist Movement are sweeping the nation. Religious Renewal is everywhere among the people.

"Thus war is averted. No National Punishment that cycle.

"But like clockwork, exactly 17 years later brings us to 1848, the high point of the Mexican War. Over 13,000 U.S. soldiers and sailors killed. Terrible disaster for the whole country. But the Battle of the Alamo set it off, so it was a war that *had* to be fought.

"Do you see how this is beyond ANY mathematical probability of merely coincidence? There is a set, immutable design at work here! And it happens to be the *exact* same one ancient Israel in the Old Testament was under. Pretty amazing, huh?"

The Federal Investigator nodded, lost in thought.

Dr. Lindsay went on, "So now, 17 years more passes, bringing us to 1865."

"The Civil War. Our nation's worst calamity," said the other man.

"Exactly," said Lindsay. "And 17 years after that, the land rests. No war in 1882 because the country had suffered enough. The past sin of slavery had been wiped out, and Reconstruction of the nation was underway. The preaching of Revivalists like D.L. Moody, Charles Spurgeon, and George Muller were everywhere, with even the White House hosting them as V.I.P.s. Religious fervor was in the air across America. Absolutely no national discipline. That Punishment Cycle was skipped entirely.

"Okay. So now, 17 years after 1882 is 1899. The Spanish-American War. Right on schedule. 17 years later is 1916, the middle of World War I, fought from

1914 to 1918. *The system is simply unfailing!*

"Note also, 17 years after that is 1933 – Not a war, but the Great Depression. Just as bad. And the date does not indicate either the beginning or the end of that national calamity, but the middle of it – when suffering of the American people was at its worst.

"17 years later was 1950."

"Hey! What happened to World War II?" asked the Investigator.

"Well, remember, this 'Plague of Locust' Schedule effects America only – no other country on earth fits into it (except modern Israel, once it was reborn). And the Second World War was not really ours. Many other countries on earth suffered much more. It was their war. Congress forced the President to stay out of it for as long as possible. We never would have gotten involved if the Empire of Japan had not foolishly attacked the U.S. Navy at Pearl Harbor. That is what made Congress finally Declare War. And even then, we only fought in the second half of the conflict.

"No, that was not our doing, and did not fit into *our* Punishment Cycle.

"But what *does* fit into it, what *our* black-eye was, our national embarrassment, was in 1950 we were in the midst of the Korean War, and losing badly. Thousands upon thousands of U.S. soldiers and sailors were perishing, and in a war we did not win. We were given a bad spanking as a nation in front of the eyes of the whole world."

"Very well," said the Fed. "Now you have my attention. Okay, what *is* going to happen next?"

The Preacher continued, "17 years after 1950 brings us to 1967, just a few years from now. I predict, with a high degree of certainty, that the current conflict in Vietnam will grow into a bigger war. And in 1967 it will be at its worst, with more American boys dying than at any other time. And because our society is growing more and more sinful, with Hippies running around like madmen everywhere, other national calamities may also result in that year – assassinations, or riots, or the like.

"Also, remember this all ties in with the new nation of Israel. In 1917 they were conceived with the Balfour Declaration. In 1950 they had just been born by declaring themselves a Sovereign State in 48, but were still effectively fighting their War of Independence two years later. And in 1967, in tandem with our own 17 Year Discipline Cycle, I predict Israel will, also, be brought into another war in the Middle East!"

"This is most interesting," said the Federal Agent. "So, Professor, if your system really works, and you can actually predict the future, then what is going to happen 17 years after that, in 1984? And 17 after that, in 2001? And 17 years later in the year 2018?"

"I can tell you *exactly* what will happen!" Dr. Lindsay quipped. "First, you and I will be long gone, sleeping six feet underground!"

"That was too easy," the other man said.

"Second, on each of those dates you just mentioned there is only one of three things that can happen, so my answer is sure, either way: Either a national spiritual renewal and repentance will be taking place and the nation will skip a punishment cycle; OR there may be at least a Christian President who believes in prayer and is doing his best to move the country in that direction, in which case the national punishment will at least be ameliorated, maybe downgraded to merely some national tragedy happening on the years in question; *OR* neither of the above will be happening at the time, in which case our sinful country will be thrust into something worse, like war.

"And some similar event, then, will also be happening in Israel on those three dates, as well."

[*Editorial Note:* We can answer the good Reverend's question precisely, from our vantage point in history in the year 2014: He was exactly correct on all counts! In 1967 the U.S. was losing thousands of Service Members in the Vietnam War, and Israel was fighting the Six Day War, in which all the Muslim nations surrounding them were trying to "wipe the Jews off the face of the earth," in their own words.

In 1984, we had the national tragedy of losing nearly 300 U.S. Marines to an Islamic Terrorist attack in Lebanon. But war, or some worse punishment, was avoided – the 17 Year Cycle was at least mitigated – because President Ronald Reagan openly professed to being a Born Again Christian, asked the nation to pray, and enacted moral laws.

In 2001, we had the national tragedy of losing nearly 5,000 innocent civilians to an Islamic Terrorist attack on New York City and Washington, D.C. But all-out war, or some worse punishment with many more dead, was avoided that year – the 17 Year Cycle was at least mitigated – because President George Bush openly professed to being a Born Again Christian, asked the nation to pray, and enacted moral laws.

In the coming target year of 2018, we may or may not be so lucky. Our nation has gone on a moral landslide over the last decade, with Hollywood force-feeding their depraved immorality down the throats of all Americans, and horrifying new laws being enacted. At this point, it does not look good for the United States that year, though whomever we elect in 2016 as the new President may help the situation.

Likewise, in Israel, the Iranian Terrorist government is rapidly building a nuclear bomb capability with which to obliterate the Jewish nation, as is their openly stated goal, so war might be forced upon them that year too, or sometime thereafter, since they have no choice but to take out the Iranian nuclear reactors themselves, since our current White House (the Obama Administration) refuses to take action against the perennial threat.]

T.L. Harlan

"And the Lord God said, 'Let there be lights in the night sky, the moon and stars, and let them be as signs and seasons for you...to reveal days and years'."

— Genesis 1:14

CHAPTER 5

The Vision

Deep of Winter, 1973. New York City near Times Square.

The Reverend David Wilkerson awoke up with a start. He sat upright in bed suddenly, and almost screamed! A cold sweat beaded on his face.

He had seen it again.

Startled, his wife lying next to him mumbled groggily, "What is it, Dave? Did you have that nightmare again?"

"I told you before, Gwen, it's not a nightmare. It is not a dream at all. It's some kind of Night *Vision,* or something. I was lying awake earlier seeing it play before my eyes for what seemed like hours. Then I guess I must have drifted off. It's just that it sometimes disturbs my sleep, too."

"Well, it's scary and I don't like it, whatever it is," she said. "This is the third night in a row, David. Just don't think about it anymore. Try to get some sleep now, Honey."

And with that, she tenderly kissed him on the cheek, turned over, and promptly resumed her slumber.

But try as he may, he could *not* stop thinking about it. Whether he closed his eyes or stared up in the darkness at the ceiling, the pictures were still there. Strange and terrible pictures. Pictures of the future of America – and the world.

Why was this happening to him? He was not a prophet! He had only had one other "vision" before in his entire life, in all the years of his Ministry. It had taken place when he was a young man. And it had come to pass exactly as he had foreseen it! It was for the founding of the Teen Challenge drug rehabilitation centers that now stretched out coast to coast across the USA, and had even gone international. This was made famous in the book *The Cross and the Switchblade,* an all-time Best Seller, which was then made into a movie starring Pat Boone and Erik Estrada.

But the startling thing that came to his mind now was the fact that this first vision of the future *had* to have been supernatural in its origin, because its predictions were ***all*** fulfilled – down to the last detail! In the natural world, the normal human brain cannot tap into the future like that.

Thinking of this, he whispered, "God help us all if this New Vision is in fact a prophetic message revealed by the Holy Spirit and is going to come to pass in America! It is too frightening to even think about.

****

In the morning, Rev. Wilkerson was up early, even with a sleepless night. In her bathrobe, Gwen walked into his study and saw him with a hot cup of coffee sitting at his typewriter. "What in the world are you doing up at this hour?" she queried.

"Three strikes and you're out!" he said. "This is the third time I have seen those future events unfold. I tell you, my wife, this is *not* my imagination! There is something unearthly at work here. I am writing it all down right now while it is still fresh in my mind."

In a few days, he finished the manuscript and sent it in to his publisher in New Jersey, the Fleming H. Revell Company, which copyrighted and printed it a few months later in 1974. This, now, is that very message from the Lord, that glimpse into the future, that warning to America, that David Wilkerson saw:

A time is coming, not immediately, but spaced out – some things not being fulfilled until 40 or more years into the future – when a Great Recession will hit the United States, and effect the whole world. It will be a time of economic confusion, beginning in Europe. Then the Stock Market in Japan will crash, and it will be followed by Wall Street shortly thereafter. Soon after that, all other nations will be pulled in and feel its effects.

Hard times are coming for Americans because of their national sins, their abandonment of God's Law when they make Man's laws. In some ways it will be as bad the Depression of the 1930s. Not just small businesses will go bankrupt, but even some major corporations will go out of business. The unemployment rate will soar. Labor Unions will be put under pressure not to call Strikes because so many workers will fear for their jobs.

The full effects of this Great Recession will not be felt until 2 or 3 years after the Stock Market initially crashes. Those who get hit the hardest will be those most in debt. Some will lose everything. Suicide rates will skyrocket. The new weapon of choice with which to commit suicide will be to overdose on drugs. That is not common now in 1973, but it will become common soon.

Around the turn of the 21st Century, the European Economic Community will develop their own money – a new kind of paper bill, which a handful of financial dictators can control the value of. When the worldwide Recession hits, many government leaders of various nations will attempt to implement a similar form of international exchange, a new form of money."

[*Editorial Note:* That is freaky incredible! How could anyone have foreseen the coming of the *Euro* and *Bitcoin* some 40 years ago? Even the prognostication concerning Hollywood movie stars and others using drug overdoses as the preferred method of suicide is uncanny. That simply was **not** the case half a century ago!]

The Vision by David Wilkerson continues:

Televangelists and "Prosperity Preachers" will likewise be thrown into confusion in the midst of this coming Great Recession. Some of them will lose so much money they will have to shut the doors of their ministry. They will have failed to show their congregations the "flip side of the coin" of the Gospel of Jesus Christ. All the "Positive Thinking" in the world cannot turn back the very hand of God, the discipline of the Almighty, chastising Unbelievers and weak-willed worldly Christians. Mega-church congregations will leave in droves, looking for more solid answers during the Hard Times. Contributions will dwindle to a trickle.

Though the riots and social unrest of the Black Community in the 1960s in this country is now a thing of the past, when this great shaking of our nation comes in the future, the rioting and looting and killings by gangs will return, even worse than before. And this time it will not be limited to disenfranchised African-Americans. I see Mexicans and other Hispanics joining in. Demonstrations in many major cities across America will turn violent and ugly. Police Departments will be overwhelmed and unable to control the rioting. Many big city Mayors will beg the Governor of their State to call in the National Guard to restore order.

When this time of trouble arrives in the USA, I also see drastic weather changes occurring and doing great damage across the country. Monster storms will cause massive flooding throughout the Southern States, but hardest hit will be the West Coast. A tragic huge loss of life will occur because of the weather gone wild. Drownings from Flash Floods and landslides will be everywhere, especially in California. This may start occurring after the U.S. Wall Street Crash.

Many Christians, wishing to be wise and make the most of their lives, will leave the Big Cities with all of their urban problems and blight, seeking a simpler lifestyle "out in the Country." They reason that if they lived in the Midwest, in the "Farming Belt," or other such rural areas of the States in which they live, when times of famine come, at least they will not starve – whether they are growing their own crops at home, or simply working on large commercial farms close by.

But I would counsel young people that even more importantly, they should invest in a sound education and choose a time-honored profession that helps people, or at least learn a skill that is truly useful in all situations and in all locations. That way, you will have the mobility to move wherever needed, whenever needed, and have a job waiting for you even when there is high unemployment.

> [*Editorial Note:* For instance, Medical Studies are never wasted. If nothing else, it teaches a person valuable survival skills. And any kind of Health Care Provider is always in high demand and receives good wages, now and into the foreseeable future. The same with many other professions. On the other hand, if you only learn to be a garbage collector or used car salesman, such unskilled labor does **not** automatically mean you will succeed financially in life, Christian or not, especially during a national Depression.]

The Vision, copyrighted in 1974, continues:

Financial advisors keep telling U.S. citizens the only thing safe to invest in is gold, and to have plenty of cash on hand before a major banking crisis like this hits. But again I would disagree. I saw gold lose its value when this international financial upheaval begins.

Though it is true that when banks suddenly go belly up, such as right after a severe Stock Market Crash like I see coming, they will cut off all credit cards—regardless of your credit worthiness—and reduce or eliminate (at least for a critical time period) the amount of money you can withdraw from your own savings and checking accounts. So, having a home safe containing some gold bullion and emergency cash to last at least 90 days or 6 months after a natural disaster, to at least pay for food and gas to get to work each day until the emergency is over, is indeed a prudent plan.

In like manner, I am not disagreeing with holding as part of your overall family savings plan physical gold and sterling silver bars and coins, to be used as emergency trading commodities if all else fails. But there are a lot of people who think that investing in gold will somehow save them – that merely owning shares in gold reserves or possessing Silver Certificates is a foolproof investment strategy that will always earn them good interest. That is what I disagree with!

I SAW IN MY VISION THAT WHEN THIS INTERNATIONAL FINANCIAL CRISIS HITS, *GOLD WILL BE DEVALUED.* Some people will lose fortunes from having their whole life savings invested only in gold.

The only thing I saw of any kind of permanent value, for the purpose of family security, is owning your own land. I don't mean property you are making monthly payments on, which the bank can simply repossess as soon as you start missing payments. I mean there is a certain amount of safety in a home that is paid off – **that you legally own, and thus cannot be evicted from.**

Nor does this mean rich people who buy investment properties will automatically be safe from losing money. When the Great Recession comes and they can no longer sell those properties in a favorable market, they may indeed lose their investment capital. I'm talking about a family having a safe place to live.

Immediately before these financial woes come upon America I felt there would be some kind of "Signs in the Sky." I'm not sure exactly what, it was unclear. Something about massive solar storms wreaking havoc on the earth, such as we have not seen now in the 20th Century, and other such celestial events.

> [*Editorial Note:* A tetrad of Blood Moons now in the 21st Century would fit this prophecy, as will happen next year in September, 2015, portending some great upheaval occurring in the 7 year period that follows that celestial event, would perhaps be germane.]

Reverend Wilkerson continues:

Far worse than a Great Recession, though, and I am not sure it will be in that same time period, is several coming "Super Quakes," which will kill over a hundred thousand people, possibly millions in total – something never before seen in American history.

They won't all happen together, but it will be very, very sad when one does occur. The disaster will be on such a large scale that it will deplete all Red Cross and FEMA emergency relief supplies and funding. Everybody expects the California Super Quake to hit, but I saw one also occurring in a part of the country not normally suspected of an active faultline. It will catch people by surprise for the most part, and thus be very terrible.

[*Editorial Note:* When David Wilkerson had this supernatural vision in 1973, the New Madrid Fault, which runs the course of the Mississippi River, and will wipe out everything from New Orleans to the Great Lakes, was not even on anyone's radar at the time, for the most part. Only a few people, other than seismologists, had even heard of it. Now, in the 21st Century, thanks to the good work of the U.S. Geological Survey, the warning is going out to local authorities from St. Louis, Missouri to Hot Springs, Arkansas to prepare for such a calamity.

The same is true for the now famous Cascadia Subduction Zone, with the USGS warning that the Washington State super-quake, when it comes, will be far worse than the California "Big One," based on the San Andreas Fault, which is estimated to only flatten everything from Los Angeles to San Francisco.]

The Vision continues:

Nothing could be worse timing than depleting FEMA emergency relief supplies and management capability after such a national emergency, because it will then make a large part of our country sitting ducks for famine – since food supplies will be sparse, and difficult to distribute to the most needy due to disrupted highway systems and roving gangs of delivery truck hijackers. This will set up the affected part of the nation for becoming vulnerable to the rampant spread of disease.

I saw in this Vision that the rapid spread of a killer virus causing a horrible epidemic was actually the greatest danger to our country. Such an international pandemic is in fact coming. It will start in the poor regions of the earth [*such as Africa*], decimating many countries, then spread here, with the capability of killing multiple thousands in its deadly wake.

[*Editorial Note:* This is truly amazing. In 1973, Rev. Wilkerson knew **nothing** of Ebola Fever, that it had a mortality rate of 80%, that there was no cure for it, that it would start in Africa, would rapidly jump borders, and would make it to the shores of the United States in just a few weeks' time from the beginning of such an outbreak. Truly a miraculous and prophetic insight!

In 2014-15, thanks to rapid mobilization on the part of the World Health Organization (funded largely by the U.S.), the world just barely missed such a modern day pandemic plague. However, what about the coming national disaster years of 2018 and 2035? What if such an epidemic were to hit us at the height of a 17 Year Punishment Cycle, if the federal government should be tapped out due to an economic crisis at home so that it could no longer fund the United Nations rapid response world health initiative? *We may not be so lucky, then!*

However, the Wilkerson Vision set no dates. Such an epidemic may wait another 17 years, not striking America until 2035, or 2052, or beyond. Indeed, since it will be an international crisis, not starting in the USA, it need not fall into one of our country's Punishment Cycles at all – which only effects America and Israel. World War II didn't, either. (Both World Wars were far worse on other countries than on us).

So, an international pandemic of Ebola or some other such Hemorrhagic Fever or the like, a modern day Black Plague, could happen at **any** time. There are no projected dates.]

David Wilkerson continues:

Why will these horrible calamities come upon America? What have we done that is so bad? The Bible is clear, such Divine retribution is visited upon certain people at certain times as a Wake Up Call – that they are doing something terribly wrong and are headed for certain destruction, IF they don't change their wicked ways!

I foresee this nation headed toward a moral landslide. It is one of the clearest things I saw in this Vision. It will in turn make us vulnerable to attacks from our enemies.

A "Flood of Filth" is coming. I predict before the end of the 20th Century certain cable channels on TV will start showing X-Rated pornographic movies. Even on network television, later at night they will show movies with topless and brief nude scenes. Liberals in the media will keep "pushing the limits" trying to get more and more immorality pumped into everyone's living rooms, to pervert the children while they are still young. Even Christians will be affected by this and suffer the consequences as well.

Even "cartoon sex" will come into vogue. Law Makers will fail in their duty of not protecting the innocent, and good decent citizens who do not want to be constantly immersed in the sexual perversions Hollywood will force down the throats of all Americans.

[*Editorial Note:* Only those of the older generation can appreciate how uncanny Rev. Wilkerson's prophecy was on this point, proving the man really did hear from the Holy Spirit and see into the future. In the early 1970s, when he had this frightening vision, people thought he was crazy. Such things could never happen. There was no such thing as the internet. There was no pornography movies shown on TV screens. There was no "cartoon sex," which is so prevalent today. Back then such things were unthinkable.]

David Wilkerson continues:

I know this sounds impossible now, but before the Judgment of God hits our country full force, even homosexuality will become popular. The Gay Movement, almost unknown now, will become so well-funded and respected that they will take over the airwaves. Popular entertainment will make socialite and comedian Gays the center of attention. Headquartered in San Francisco, they will become so militant and brazen they will even flaunt their detestable sin openly on network Talk Shows. Christians will hesitate to speak out against them for fear of being accused of "intolerance."

I realize most people now in 1973 cannot envision something like this happening in America, and think I surely must be wrong on this point, but I was shown clearly by the Lord that the horrible and unnatural sin of sodomy would not only be legalized, but would become acceptable and fashionable by the wealthy elite in the entertainment industry right before the hammer of God's justice came smashing down on our nation!

[*Editorial Note:* Wow! No editorial comment from me! The editor of this book is too afraid of being labeled "intolerant" if I say a word on this subject.]

The Vision, copyrighted 1974, continues:

And the heterosexual "sex perverts" growing more bold in American society are just as bad. I predict that before the end of the 20th Century, **the U.S. will become the largest purveyor of pornography in the world!** And not just being produced in Tinsel Town, but throughout the country.

The sex perverts will go after younger and younger girls, until something called "Child Pornography" develops. These Child Molesters will be deviant sex addicts who will actually rape children and babies and videotape it for the enjoyment of others! It is a severe form of mental illness from which there is no return. These inhuman monsters will then often kidnap or kill their victims afterward, to hide the crime.

Pedophilia is an addiction straight out of Hell! But mark my words, though it is impossible to believe now, one day it will run rampant across America!

Illegal drug and narcotic addiction will likewise become worse, growing in number of users to unbearable levels throughout society. They will developed new and ever more powerful types of drugs that once addicted to, the habit can no longer be broken by the human will. I foresee our future Law Makers lacking the moral courage and intestinal fortitude to stem the tide of this national epidemic. The politicians will fail in their primary responsibility of protecting the American People from these horrors.

The Holy Bible warns, "Be not deceived, God is not mocked; whatsoever a man soweth, that also shall he reap." So, when you see all these things coming about in the News, know that God's Judgment is about to descend upon us as a nation.

And it will be deserved.

"He that being often reproved, hardeneth his neck, shall suddenly be destroyed, and that without remedy."

-- Proverbs 29:1

CHAPTER 6

The Highest Law in the Land

Why are the 17 Year Locust Plagues against Israel in the Bible now against America as well?

What has the United States done to deserve the wrath of Almighty God?

Why these discipline cycles of national punishment every 17 years, like no other country on earth receives, other than modern Israel?

The federal legal rulings handed down by the United States Supreme Court, the Highest Law of the Land explain why:

1. The U.S. Government decides Black Americans are allowed to be slaves. Slavery and the owning of another person based on the color of their skin is lawful. Why? Because they are just "property." If they displease their Master, he can simply kill them, and it is not a crime. Why is it lawful for African-Americans to be treated this way? Because they are not allowed to be U.S. Citizens. Why? Because, based on Evolutionary Theory propounded by Darwin, THEY ARE NOT FULLY HUMAN! According to the U.S. Supreme Court, a person of color is only 3/5th of a

human being! (Dred Scott vs. Sanford, 1857).

2. In a similar landmark decision, the U.S. Supreme Court also ruled all women can be robbed of their rights guaranteed under the U.S. Constitution if they meet one condition. Any female resident of the United States can be denied the right to Life, Liberty, and the Pursuit of Happiness as long as she is pre-born. One day before her mother's due date, she can be gruesomely and painfully murdered while still living in the protection of the womb. Though she has been alive for nine months, and can fully feel pain and fear in a fully developed human body and mind, her parents can legally have her arms and legs cut off of her torso with a sharp knife, by a sociopathic butcher pretending to be a doctor, as the innocent little victim screams and screams in agonizing pain and terror, which **ultrasound photographs verify happens during an abortion.**

If the baby displeases her mother, she can simply have her killed one day before her birth and it is not a crime. Why? Because she is just "property." How is it lawful for pre-born women to be treated this way? Because they are not allowed to be U.S. Citizens. Why? Because, based on Evolutionary Theory propounded by Darwin, THEY ARE NOT FULLY HUMAN! According to the U.S. Supreme Court, a pre-born person is not a human being! (Roe vs. Wade, 1973).

3. Even after finally granting African-Americans U.S. Citizenship and illegalizing slavery, the High Court bypasses the authority of Congress and makes it federal law that People of Color can be segregated

from "civilized society" and kept from eating, living, or going to school near the rest of their fellow Americans. The Supreme Court reasons, "Any supposed discrimination exists only in the minds of the Black Community." (Pace vs. Alabama, 1883)

4. The Highest Law in the Land next rules that a man cannot choose for himself any wife he wants – if she is of a different ethnicity. The Federal Supreme Court says it is illegal for a woman to live with her husband in this country, if his skin color is a different shade. The Justices reason the average American citizen should not be trusted with such decision-making power. Those decisions over their personal lives must only be made by the Government. (Plessy vs. Ferguson, 1896)

5. The crime of sodomy is no longer a crime. Homosexuality is no longer deviant, or even aberrant, sexual behavior. It does not matter that the Bible, the Word of God, warns strictly against such sinful behavior, in both the Old Testament and New Testament. It does not matter what the laws have always been from the founding of the country. It does not matter what State Laws rule on sodomite crimes against others, they will be overturned and dictated by the federal Supreme Court instead. The will of the citizens no longer counts. (Lawrence vs. Texas, 2003)

6. Marriage is no longer between one man and one woman. The U.S. Supreme Court rules Gay Marriages are now legal, and all citizens MUST recognize them and cooperate with them, or else they will be guilty of a crime and punished under the law. An American is

no longer allowed to follow his or her conscience or Religion in the United States. It does not matter what the moral laws have always been from the founding of the country. It does not matter what good State Laws may rule against Same-Sex Marriages, they will be overturned and dictated by the Federal Supreme Court instead. The will of the citizens does not matter.

Christians and Jews who follow their religious or moral convictions, and do not want to have their businesses support Sodomite "weddings," will henceforth be arrested and jailed as criminals. Thus rules the gods and goddesses of the United States Supreme Court, who will not allow the old God to have any say in the matter any longer. The Lord God of the Bible is henceforth banished from this country. (*cf.,* Obergefell vs. Hodges, 2015).

7. Praying to that odious God of the Bible is now illegal, on public property across the land. The right of Americans to pray freely to their God is hereby abolished by the Supreme Court if those citizens don't meet federal qualifications. The qualification is they must not be a school student. Students are henceforth forbidden to read the Bible or pray while in school. Prayer is now against the law in the country that was built on prayer. (Engel vs. Vitale, 1962).

8. The sins of adultery and fornication are no longer forbidden, but are now lawful. The U.S. Supreme Court makes the practice of cheating on your wife or husband the permissible Law of the Land. Women's former Rights to have the law protect them if their husband commits adultery are hereby

abrogated by the High Court. A woman henceforth has no right to appeal to the Law for help in holding her family together, nor a husband and father attempting to do the same. (Griswold vs. Connecticut, 1965 / Eisenstadt vs. Baird, 1972).

Meanwhile, sacred Scripture, the very Word of God says:

"Be not deceived; God is not mocked: for whatsoever a man soweth that shall he also reap. For he that soweth to the flesh shall of the flesh reap corruption." (Galatians 6:7)

"The wicked shall be turned into Hell, as will the nation that ignores God." (Psalm 9:17 KJV)

"The nation that chooses wickedness travels down the Road to the Grave. All nations that forget the Fear of the Lord, the God of Israel, shall meet their destruction."

— Prophecy from the Book of Psalms
(Ps. 9:18, Eastern Orthodox Septuagint Bible)

CHAPTER 7

The Silent Scream

January 22, 1973. "A Date that will live in Infamy."

She was the *Delight of her Daddy.*

He longed for her to come to their home so he could cuddle her, and curl her golden locks with his fingers, and stroke her dainty cheeks, oh so gently, till she fell asleep in his arms.

But Mommy wanted to hold her tight, and squeeze her until she giggled, and tickle her tummy in endless fits of laughter every time she changed her diapers. She was already the *Pride of her Mother*, the first-fruit of an athletic and healthy body she had been blest with.

Grandma longed only to hold her: To once again feel a warm, sleeping baby's breath on her shoulder. Just one more time to feel the tiny, delicate hands clenching and unclenching her finger in wonderment. She was the *Hope of her Grandmother.*

In fact, Grandma had already spoiled her, even before she arrived. She had bought miniature pink dresses with white silk ruffles, and brought home baby-boxes of baby-soft baby blankets, and warm woolen mittens and socks, and brightly colored plastic rattles, and red and yellow and blue striped rubber balls. Grandma just wanted to hold the new Bundle of Joy, and couldn't wait until she got there. Her soft and happy coos and gurgles she knew would somehow comfort the old woman... and fill her with hope.

Daddy had already bought her a little bike, which looked like it was meant for a doll; and a tiny table and dinette set, which were meant for a doll.

"Don't be ridicules," the baby heard Mommy's muffled voice say. "It will be years before our daughter can use those!"

But he didn't listen to her.

He went right on assembling the bike. He even dragged a box from the garage into the backyard and erected a miniature swing set there under the new peach tree.

"You're so silly, Reginald!" Mommy said to him. But she gave her husband a big kiss on the cheek when she said it.

Baby was happy in her own little Baby World. She was warm, nursed, comfy, and could eat as much as she wanted as often as she wanted. Lying there in the quiet peacefulness of her oft rocking cradle, she had just eaten, gone potty, and now felt relieved, and quite contented.

The doctor had seen her earlier that day, (but he looked at Mommy first), and his medical diagnosis was that the tyke was nourished, developing nicely, full of energy, in the pink of health, and (frankly) the little plumpling was quite well-fed! He prescribed some more of the same vitamins for Mommy to keep taking, and asked if her morning-sickness had gone away, which it had.

While the kindly old General Practitioner watched Baby through an ultrasound fluoroscope, she thought she would show off a bit and did a jig for him.

"Oh, look!" she heard his voice far away cry with delight to Mommy, "The little rascal is dancing for us!" And they both laughed.

She couldn't understand their words, of course, not knowing English yet, (being only 8 months old), but she laughed right along with them anyway.

A Silent Laugh.

That night, she went to sleep quite satisfied with herself and the day's activities, and sighed contentedly.

A Silent Sigh.

But in Baby's warm, soft, dark world there was one problem... She could not understand danger. She had never known want, nor felt pain before, so she was equally incapable of comprehending the concept of Evil. No one had ever hurt her, so she was oblivious to the fact that there was even such a thing as "danger" in the big world Outside; or that there were evil people who could harm her if she were not protected by her parents.

That is why she was so surprised and shocked when, a couple of weeks later, she felt a deep foreboding suddenly come upon her. Like all humans, regardless of age or location, she had the spiritual ability to sense imminent danger approaching, even though she could not fully comprehend what that meant at this tender age in her young life. She only knew it filled her with dread and fear, a new and unbearable emotion for her.

She had been half-asleep, contentedly sucking her

thumb, when this horrible feeling came upon her again. Now she suddenly awoke fully and sat up, crying out for her mother though unable to make a sound. But this time her mother did not begin rocking her and talk comfortingly to her, as usual. She could not even hear her reassuring muffled voice in the darkness. Where was she? Where did she go?

"Mommy? Mommy? Where are you? Why won't you answer? What is wrong? You are not mad at me are you, Mommy? Have *I* done something wrong?

The baby began to get more frightened. Nothing like this had ever happened before.

Where was Daddy? She couldn't hear his voice, either. Where could they have gone? They wouldn't just leave her there in the darkness, all by herself, would they? What if they never came back! What if she could never be with them again!

Now she *really* began to get scared. At just the thought of this, she began crying her heart out. But her parents didn't respond to her heart-breaking sobs.

Silent Sobs.

For God's sake, were they even still alive?

Suddenly, she felt an alien presence near her! She stopped crying, frozen with fear. She could see nothing in the blackness all about her, but definitely felt the motion of an intruder go by. A cold, dark, alien intruder. She was too shocked to move. But somehow she knew... it was looking for *her!*

In shear panic she began crying out, in incomprehensible baby shrieks that only her ears could hear or understand, "Mommy! Mommy! Help! There is a Stranger in here! Come and rescue me! Mommy? Daddy? Help me, please! I'm scared to death—

THERE IS AN INVADER IN THE SANCTUARY!!

"I know I must have done something terribly wrong for you to be so mad at me, and not come to my aid. But, please, *please,* don't desert me now... Not now, in my greatest hour of need!

Then, she felt the icy-cold Alien right next to her... It had found her! She screamed in terror!

A Silent Scream.

Suddenly, from out of nowhere, a silver knife blade lunged at the baby! She of course was unable to leap out of the way, so the razor-sharp point sliced her flesh down one side.

"Ow! Ow! The pain! Mommy, help me! Won't somebody – anybody – please help me?" she screamed over and over again. Never had she felt such searing, burning pain!

And Jesus groaned in agony on the Cross.

The knife came from out of the darkness again at the defenseless child. She could do nothing, but shriek in horror and kick wildly. This time the evil silver blade cut deep into her leg, slicing it to the bone. Blood spurted out of the severed artery from her tiny racing heart.

"Mommy!! Daddy!! For Heaven's sake, come and help me!

I beg of you! What did I do that was so bad? I'm sorry I did it, whatever it was! I'm sorry I was such a bad girl...

I'm so sorry. But *please* forgive me! In the Name of

God's, if there is even an ounce of mercy left in you, save me *now*— Quickly, before it's too late!!!

And Jesus wept.

But still her parents did not come to rescue her. The baby was smeared with bright red blood everywhere. She tried her hardest to roll out of the way each time the wicked, blood-splattered razor came after her, time after time, fighting valiantly to hold onto *Life.*

But it finally caught her again, this time slicing off one of her arms, breaking the tiny bones.

And Jesus writhed in the excruciating pain of the crucifixion.

"MOMMY, WHERE *ARE* YOU?!! I know I was a terribly bad girl. But I'm so sorry...

"Won't *somebody* please help me? GOD, SAVE ME!"

The pain and horror were unbearable. The unbelievably evil knife attacker now chopped off both the baby's arms and legs so she couldn't even thrash about anymore. She began chocking in her own blood, lying there gasping without air, as the life slowly ebbed out of her little body.

And Jesus hung on the Cross, bleeding from the painful nail-wounds dug deep into His tender flesh, as the life slowly bled out of Him.

But what she heard next, as she lay there dying,

was more horrible than she could bear. It was the sheer magnitude of the evil of it, more than her comprehension could fathom, that drove her to fresh tears and wailing. For she heard the voice of a *Traitor...* A traitor more trusted, and thus more treacherous, than Judas Iscariot himself.

It was the cold and unfeeling voice of her own mother.

"Ouch, that hurt," it said. "Will you hurry up, Doctor! "

"Just a few more incisions, and then the suction tube, and that should do it," someone new answered. His voice was mechanical and hard-hearted.

In utter horror and disbelief, the little girl baby cried out, "How could you call yourself my *Mother,* you traitor! And how could that *butcher* call himself a physician? He has turned the *Hippocratic Oath* into a *Hypocritic Oath.* And where was my dear *father* when I needed him more than ever to exercise his primary responsibility in life of protecting *me?"*

He was, in fact, at home— watching TV (because an important soccer game was on that day).

Her dying thoughts were, "I loved you with all my little heart. And this is how you return my love? By dumping me in a garbage pail, torn limb from limb? What kind of parents are you? What kind of *monsters* are you!"

She sobbed and sobbed, until her little unborn heart broke.

And Jesus wept.

****

After it was all over, Grandma disagreed with their decision – Something about genetic tests showed the child might be born with a handicap, or something. (It didn't really matter *what* the excuse was). Disappointedly, the old woman took back the tiny pink dresses and baby-soft blankets, and once again returned them to the moth balls of her ancient cedar chest from another era.

The miniature bike sat untouched in the very back of the garage, and just gathered dust over the years.

And though the peach tree in the backyard grew big and old, waiting in vain for little children to one day play in the grass underneath its shady boughs, the small swing-set next to it remained unused and unseen, year after year, until it simply rusted into oblivion.

"The wicked descend down into the bowels of Hell, along with the nations that forget God."

-- Psalm 9:17

CHAPTER 8

The Prophet

July 4th, 1954. Manhattan Island, New York.

Alonso Allen was a Native American, and a troubled teenager. His father was an alcoholic. And he, as well, had a weakness for the White Man's fire-water. Mean people referred to him as "the Drunk Indian," and "Half-Breed." Prison was in his future.

But when he was 23 years old he had a conversion experience and became a Born Again Christian. That changed everything. His life took a dramatic turn for the better. He eventually graduated from Bible College in Missouri, got married, and became a Pentecostal Minister.

Reverend A.A. Allen continued to succeed until he was promoted to Pastor of a large Assembly of God church in Corpus Christi, Texas. After that, he met Oral Roberts, and in time became a famous International Evangelist himself. Thousands of Christians testified over the years that he was truly gifted with the power of the Holy Spirit. He was neither a religious fake nor a weird-o.

On the 4th of July, 1954, Rev. Allen was on top of the Empire State Building viewing the Statue of

Liberty through a telescope. Suddenly, a Divine Vision came upon him. This was highly unusual. But he remembered the words of the Bible, "And it shall come to pass in the Last Days, saith the Lord, that I will pour out My Spirit upon all flesh: And your young men shall see visions, and your old men shall dream dreams." (Acts 2:1).

Afterward, he explained to people the details of this experience thusly:

Suddenly I heard the voice of the Lord. It was as clear and distinct as a human voice. But I knew it had come from Heaven. The voice repeated the message spoken to ancient Israel by the Prophet, "The eyes of the Lord range to and fro throughout the whole earth, to show Himself strong on behalf of them whose heart is pure toward Him. Herein thou hast done foolishly, O Israel. Therefore, from henceforth thou shalt have wars." (II Chron. 16:9)

As I looked through the telescope, suddenly the Spirit of God came upon me in a way I had never experienced before. I was enabled to see things far beyond the range of the telescope. It was no longer Manhattan Island that I saw, but a far larger view – across the whole country. The entire North American continent was spread out before me like a map on a table. In the Natural Order, from up there one could only see from the East River to the Hudson River. But now, in the Supernatural Order, I could see from the Atlantic Ocean to the Pacific Ocean!

Instead of the Statue of Liberty standing there in the bay in New York Harbor, I now saw her standing far out by the Gulf of Mexico. So I realized this indeed was a Divine Vision meant to show me the future of America. I was neither dreaming nor in a trance, but wide awake. I did not see these unfolding scenes "in my mind," but with my actual eyes. I was excited by this unusual experience, but also a bit startled. So, to prove it to myself, I took my eye away from the telescope lens for a moment. Yet the same scene remained spread out before me.

[*Editorial Note:* This is one of the tests experts use to authenticate an actual supernatural vision, as opposed to a mere natural "waking dream," or a drug induced hallucination, etc.]

Reverend Allen continues:

There, clear and distinct, lay all of North America with all its great cities. To the north lay the Great Lakes. Close by in the northeast was New York State. I could see Seattle, Washington and Portland, Oregon far out in the northwest. Down the West Coast were San Francisco and Los Angeles. Closer in the foreground, I saw New Orleans near the center of the Gulf Coast area. The great towering Rocky Mountain range was in view, and I could trace with my eye the Continental Divide.

Suddenly, from the sky I saw a giant hand coming down! That gigantic hand was reaching out toward the Statue of Liberty. Her gleaming torch was torn from her hand by it, and in it instead was placed a wine goblet. And I saw protruding from that great cup, a sword shining with a glistening light. Never before had I seen such a sharp, dangerous, threatening blade.

Then, I heard a voice from Heaven, saying, "Thus saith the Lord of Hosts, 'Drink and get drunk. Vomit, and fall to your knees, never to rise again! This, because of the sword which I will send against you'."

As I heard these words, I recognized them as being similar to a verse from the Prophet Jeremiah against the nation of Israel when it had drifted into sin. (Jer. 20:7). I was amazed to hear the Statue of Liberty speak out in reply, "No, I will not drink of it!"

Then, sounding like thunder, I heard again the voice of the Lord saying, "YE SHALL CERTAINLY DRINK." (Jeremiah 25:28.)

Suddenly the giant hand forced the blood-red cup to the lips of Lady Liberty, and she became powerless to defend herself. The mighty hand of God forced her to drink every drop! As she drank the bitter dregs, these were the words I heard, "'Should ye, among all nations, be left unpunished? Ye shall not! For I shall call for a sword upon all the inhabitants of the earth,' saith the Lord of Hosts." (Jeremiah 25:29).

When the wine goblet was withdrawn from the lips of the Statue of Liberty, I noticed that sharp and deadly dagger was missing from the cup, which could only mean one thing: She had been forced to drink it. And I realized the sword always symbolizes war, death, and destruction, which is no doubt on the way in retribution for our national sins.

Then, as one drunken on liquor or drugs, I saw the Statue of Liberty become unsteady on her feet and begin to stagger and lose her balance. I saw her splashing into the Gulf of Mexico, trying to regain her balance. She staggered again and again until she fell to her knees. As I watched her desperate attempts to regain her balance, and rise again to her feet, my heart was moved with pity and compassion for her struggles. I wondered if Lady Liberty would ever be able to stand again. As she lay there, I had an overwhelming desire to reach out my hand and keep her head above water, for I knew that if she stay that way, she would drown there off the shores of Mexico.

[*Editorial Note:* In symbolic terminology, this appears to indicate U.S. troubled relations with Mexico, leading to a national catastrophe. In 1954, when A.A. Allen was granted this revelation (and it was immediately put into print in various publications that next year), such a thing would have been nearly impossible on the international scene. But now, in 2014, as this book (containing a reprint of the original story) finally goes to print after having initially been written nearly half a century ago, Americans are just starting to wake up to the reality of what kind of horrendous problems an uncontrolled and unenforced immigration policy toward Mexico can cause.

It is not exaggerating to say that if left unchecked, the growing illegal alien problem can and will literally bankrupt the U.S. socio-economic infrastructure, especially in the Southern States.

This is neither racist nor alarmist to say, as even Hispanic American Senators, Congressmen, and other Federal Government Officials, some of whom are now running for President of the United States, openly admit. The editor of this publication is himself the son of an immigrant. My mother and grandparents literally "got off the boat" at Ellis Island, right where this story takes place, and couldn't even speak English when they arrived – being political refugees during the World War.

Plus, my wife and in-laws are Spanish, coming from Latin America, also political refugees. So, it hurts me to have to report this sad news on this subject.

But we must face the facts.

The reality is, since America is headed for another "Divine Punishment Cycle" (as elsewhere explained in this book), beginning sometime after Yom Kippur of the Hebrew calendar (the Jewish High Holy Day) next year – that is, after 23 September 2015, or after the mitigating Year of Jubilee that follows it in 2016, (that means, starting in 2017), and will reach its apogee during the year 2018 (the time when America will suffer the most), some experts calculate this could be tied in with the current invasion of illegal aliens flooding over the border from Mexico.

For example, the USA (and much of the rest of the world) "dodged the bullet" in the recent Ebola Epidemic, since the World Health Organization – due to many heroic doctors and nurses risking their own lives – was able to contain it... THIS TIME. But we may not be so lucky in the near future.

Another outbreak, if in a country ripe for exploitation by the virus, such as Mexico, will quickly overwhelm their medical facilities. When the Mexicans realize their government can't (or won't) help them, and they understand the epidemic will catch like wildfire and rapidly turn into a national pandemic – and that Ebola Fever kills over three-quarters of the people who contract it, and is a disease worse than the Black Plague that decimated Europe in the Dark Ages, logical projections dictate a high probability many Mexicans will flee north as quickly as they can, in an attempt to cross the border by any means possible to get to the relative safety of U.S. Health Care Facilities.

They will simply swarm the border, overrunning every check-point crossing from California to Texas, and invade the country en masse! What are the U.S. Border Agents supposed to do? The handful of Officers there at each station can arrest hundreds each night, but only while **thousands** push past them and run north into hiding under cover of darkness.

And even if the then President of the Untied States activates the National Guard to secure our borders and patrol them, what are they supposed to do? Shoot hundreds of innocent men, women, and children who are rushing past them in a panic? The American news media covering such a nightly massacre of unarmed civilians would not stand for it, and the American people watching such a heartbreaking scene won't be able to stomach it.

Therefore, the end result will inevitably be not thousands, but millions, of illegal Mexicans swarming over the U.S. border, many of whom could be Ebola carriers!

This is a frightening and alarming scenario, and needs to be taken as the serious threat that it could become in the near future. But it does NOT necessarily mean this projection is set in stone. The Future is liquid. It can always be changed. Free Will is never impaired. Protective measures **could** be taken in advance to prevent this scenario from ever occurring on American soil— such as building a Border Wall.]

The Allen Prophecy continues:

Then, as I watched, another amazing thing was taking place. Far to the northwest, coming from beyond Alaska, [from Siberia and Russia and the Slavic nations, the former Soviet Union] a huge, black cloud was arising. As it rose, it was as black as night. It seemed to be in the shape of a man's head. As it continued to rise, I could see the ominous black cloud was taking the shape of a skull. Then the boney shoulders began to appear, and on either side, long bone arms.

I still saw North America spread out like a map on a table, only now this terrible skeleton was slowly rising from behind it. At the waist, the giant monster bent toward the United States, stretching out one boney hand toward the east and one towards the west – [one pointing toward New York City and one toward Seattle.]

As the awful form stretched forward, I could see that its entire attention seemed to be focused upon the United States, overlooking Canada. As it reached down toward Chicago, and looked out toward both coasts, I knew its one interest was to destroy multitudes of people. [It was a maleficent Angel of Death.]

As I watched in horror, the titanic black cloud stopped just above the Great Lakes region, and turned its face toward New York. Then out of the horrible, great, gaping mouth began to appear billows of smoke, as a cigarette smoker would blow puffs out. These whitish vapors were being blown to hover over New York City. Then the smoke began to spread until it covered all of the Eastern Seaboard, down to Washington, D.C.

[*Editorial Note:* Though this revelation occurred a half century BEFORE the Muslim Terrorist attacks on the Twin Towers in New York City and the Pentagon in Washington, D.C., on September 11, 2001, two things should be noted: The smoke seen in the vision certainly fits what was actually seen that terrible day in those two U.S. target cities, in which the entire Eastern Seaboard was indeed affected. And if Reverend Allen were indeed being shown an authentic vision of the future of America by the Holy Spirit, then the three puffs of smoke enumerated below perfectly fit in with the "Divine Punishment Cycles" (elsewhere explained in this book) of the fateful years 2001, 2018, 2035, etc.]

The Prophecy continues:

After this, there was a second blow against the USA as the Skeleton of Death turned westerly. Out of the horrible mouth and nostrils came another great puff of foul smoke. This time it was blown in the direction of the West Coast. In a few moments, the entire Pacific Coast was covered with its deadly vapors – [from Hollywood, to Los Angeles, to San Francisco, to Seattle.]

[*Editorial Note:* If the first blow (against the East Coast) occurred in 2001, then there is a chance the second blow (against the West Coast) may occur in one of the next 17 Year National Punishment Cycles, in 2018, 2035, or 2052, though this is not immutable – it may skip a cycle, as has happened before in history.

But if it does happen then, it makes it much more likely that the third blow (against New

Orleans, St. Louis, and the middle of the country – probably the coming New Madrid Super Quake) will occur the next 17 Year Cycle, in the year 2035, or 2052, etc.

Most readers are no doubt aware there is an ominous alignment of the cities mentioned above, in the Skull's second blow against America, as they are all right along the Pacific Rim (part of the so called "Ring of Fire"), conjoining California's infamous San Andreas Fault with Washington's less well-known, but infinitely more dangerous, Cascadia Subduction Zone. (That is the one the U.S. Geological Survey is far more frightened of).

The sad truth is, when the "Big One" hits Los Angeles, and destroys Hollywood for its sins – especially for shoving the unnatural and heinous sin of sodomy down the throats of all descent and moral Americans, making Christians look like **they** are the bad guys for simply telling the truth of the Bible concerning homosexuality – this occurring at the southern end of the faultline, then as the Super Quake travels north and flattens San Francisco (and all it stands for) along the way, because San Andreas and Cascadia are along the edge of the same subterranean tectonic plate, it means Oregon and Washington will likely also be hit at the same time, though seismologists currently are not certain the L.A. earthquake will set off the Seattle quake. Hopefully it won't. The horrendous Death Toll will be bad enough in California alone.

What FEMA is certain of, though, is the coming Cascadia Super Quake—whenever it **does** hit—will be far worse than the San

Andreas "Big One." The Federal Emergency Management Agency of the U.S. Government predicts when Seattle goes down there will be millions more people killed in Washington and Oregon than in the California super quake, whether they occur simultaneously or not.

Both the author of this book and his wife have all their brothers and sisters and adult children living in this West Coast Danger Zone. So, like many others, we are hoping and praying that this major calamity will not occur anytime soon, but will wait until the year 2035 or later, instead. However, as this publication is being rushed to print, the U.S. Supreme Court has just foolishly and sinfully legalized homosexual marriage, making a mockery of the Sacrament of Holy Matrimony, thus setting up our nation for a very big fall. A very big fall indeed!

But regardless of when this natural disaster occurs, the loss of life is going to be devastating to the whole country. When it happens, hopefully our politicians will finally get the message from God, and restore Judeo-Christian moral laws to this land so we can avoid further National Punishment Cycles in the future.]

The Allen Prophecy continues:

Finally, as a third and final blow against our nation, a great puff of this smoke of destruction was blown toward the middle of the country. As I watched, St. Louis and Kansas City were enveloped in these deadly vapors. It kept heading south until it came to New Orleans, then swept down until it reached the Statue of Liberty where she stood staggering drunkenly in the blue waters of the Gulf of Mexico. As the stinking white vapors began to spread around the head of

Lady Liberty, she took in one gasping breath then began to cough as though to rid her lungs of the horrible fumes she had inhaled. One could readily discern by the painful coughing that those acrid vapors had seared her lungs.

She fell face forward into the waters of the Gulf, and lay still – as still as death.

And tears began to roll down my face.

[*Editorial Note:* When A.A. Allen had this vision, he wondered if this might not portend some future nerve gas or mustard gas attack by the Soviet Union against the U.S.A. Though that is certainly possible, our intrepid preacher was unaware that he described the exact location of the New Madrid Faultline, which runs from Lake Michigan in the north, follows the Mississippi River south, past St. Louis, and ends up in New Orleans and the Gulf of Mexico, cutting our nation in half, east and west.

In 1954 when this vision occurred, there was no FEMA nor any modern seismologists warning of the coming New Madrid super-quake, which the federal government says is already overdue. The only question now is, will it happen during the 2035 cycle, or 17 years thereafter in 2052? Or 17 years later in 2069?]

Reverend Allen continues:

As I sat quietly weeping for the fallen Statue of Liberty, suddenly the screaming of sirens shattered the silence. The wailing sirens [of the Early Warning System] seemed to scream, "RUN FOR YOUR LIVES!" Never before had I heard such a shrill, screeching sound. They were everywhere around the country - to the north, the south, the east and the west - multitudes of sirens, all going off simultaneously. It was terrifying!

I saw people everywhere running. But none of them got very far before they fell. Millions of people across the land were falling in the streets, on the sidewalks, struggling. I heard their screams for mercy and help. I heard their horrible coughing, as though their lungs had been seared with fire. I heard the moanings and groanings of the doomed and dying as they lay beneath collapsed buildings. It was terrible!

As I watched, I observed that there were a few wise Americans who did make it to protective shelters, which had been readied in advance for this very purpose. But only a few ever got to these bomb-shelters.

Then suddenly, I saw from the Atlantic and from the Pacific and out of the Gulf, rocket-like objects that seemed to come up like fish leaping out of the water. High into the air they leaped, each headed in a different direction, but every one toward the United States. On the ground, the sirens screamed louder. And up from the ground I saw similar slender rockets [missiles] beginning to ascend. To me, these appeared to be interceptor rockets, although they arose from different points all over the United States. However, very few of them seemed to be successful in intercepting the enemy missiles that had risen from the ocean on every side.

These defensive rockets finally reached their maximum height, slowly turned over, and fell back toward the earth in defeat. Then suddenly, the missiles that had leaped out of the oceans like fish, all hit land and exploded at the same time in a coordinated attack. The explosions were earsplitting, unlike anything ever before seen in warfare. The next thing which I saw was a huge, a gigantic, ball of fire rising up high into the sky. The only thing I have ever seen that resembles what I saw in my vision was a picture in the newspaper of the explosion of the H-bomb being tested somewhere in the South Pacific some months ago. In my vision, it was so real I seemed to feel a searing heat from it. These landed all across the USA, on every major city, burning them to the ground.

Then, everything went dark.

[*Editorial Note:* This portion of Rev. Allen's vision is what caused even the skeptics to perk up and take notice, making it go viral internationally. That is because there are several testing points, several historical items of interest, that have already come to pass which no person living in 1954 when he saw these things would have had any idea were going to appear in the future. It was humanly impossible to predict, given the technology of that day, and is very strong evidence that these revelations were indeed Divinely given as an authentic look into the future, probably a century or more in advance, rather than just the crazed ramblings of an itinerant preacher. This has all the hallmarks of an accurate prophetic warning to a specially chosen nation.

First, remember this vision was immediately put into print just a few months after it occurred, by several publications, so there is no way anyone could go back later and "cheat" by changing the text. Second, the Intercontinental Ballistic Missiles carrying nuclear weapons he saw did not exist in 1954. The first prototype was test launched in 1957, three years after the vision, and not even operational with a warhead until 1959. Even then, the Soviet Union did not develop an arsenal of them that could be launched from Russia and reach U.S. shores until a decade later. (That is why they needed to place them in Communist Cuba, their allies, just 90 miles off the Florida coast, in the early 1960s during the Cuban Missile Crisis).

Third, they were seen doing something utterly impossible for that day: The ICBM missiles were coming from under the water, leaping out of the sea like flying fish, from launch points all over the oceans surrounding CONUS. That is a common expectation today in warfare, but **in 1954 there were no nuclear submarines!**

The first one was invented by the U.S. Navy, the *USS Nautilus*, and not put into service until 1955. And even then, it could not launch an ICBM with an atomic warhead. The Soviets did not develop a fleet of such nuclear subs with that kind of capability, to make what was seen even a possibility, until the next decade. **That is a hallmark of supernatural knowledge being revealed in advance.**

Fourth, American civilians hearing sirens and running for bomb shelters sounds to us in modern times also like an expected part of warfare. But that was very unusual at the time this vision occurred. Such a network of privately owned bomb shelters across the land did not exist in the USA until the Cuban Missile Crisis in the 1960s, nearly a decade later. And though military installations in this country had emergency sirens in 1954, as well as civilian fire departments, and the British had developed such a national warning system during World War II for themselves, our own U.S. Ballistic Early Warning System was not deployed to protect CONUS until the mid-1960s, also thanks to the Cuban Missile Crisis, which seemed to finally wake Americans up to the reality of the danger.

Today we are so used to hearing that network of sirens across the continent being tested once a month along with the Emergency Broadcasting System that we take it for granted. But it was not always that way, and in 1954 was not a detail a normal citizen would even think of, especially not a non-governmental civilian like Rev. Allen who had never seen nor heard any such thing.

And fifth, how could this modern prophet also have foreseen the failure of the interceptor rockets the U.S. was using as a defensive measure? NORAD was not developed to perform such a task until the 1960s. And it was not until the 1970s we found out the whole system was ineffective and would have been an abysmal failure if we had ever needed to launch such a missile defense. The original weaponry was dismantled, and subsequently President Ronald Reagan had to beg Congress to fund his Strategic Defense Initiative in the 1980s to replace it, instead. Evidently, whatever we have in place in the future when this occurs will likewise be as ineffective.

Hopefully, this World War III scenario of nuclear destruction in CONUS from a massive and coordinated Russian submarine fleet missile attack will not occur in the next 17 year Punishment Cycle after that third blow against our country, that is, in the year 2052. There is nothing that says it has to be. It may be an event for the more distant future.

Plus, nothing is set in concrete. We can always change our destiny. The future is in a liquid state and can be altered by what we do now. It is always changing, affected by various decisions of various national governments. **Only the prophecies of the Bible will for sure come to pass, exactly as predicted.** (That is a promise of the Word of God in Habakkuk 2:3, that they will indeed happen, as God's plans cannot be thwarted by Man).

But the USA and Canada and England are not mentioned in any Biblical prophecies, at least not directly. So, we are a wildcard. We can go in either direction. It is all up to the will of our people, and our ability to force our government leaders to take proper action, to protect our country. American history shows that when we are in a time of national repentance, or religious revival, the 17 Year Locust Plague punishments can be skipped for one cycle or more.

If our citizens will realize the destructive negative forces currently being unleashed on society, such as the murder of millions of innocent little babies while still in the womb, or legalizing sodomy and Gay Marriage, or continuing to allow pornography to be legal – which leads to vast increases in prostitution, child molestation, kidnappings, and Kiddie Porn – and will turn away from those sins and enact **good** laws instead, protecting the rights of Christians, Jews, and all other moral people, then we can avoid Divine Retribution—or at least delay it—so that national calamities do NOT occur in the target years of 2018, or 2035, or 2052, etc.]

The Allen Prophecy concludes:

After that, there came to my ears another sound – a sound of distant singing. It was the sweetest music I ever heard! There was joyful shouting, and sounds of happy laughter. Immediately, I knew it was the rejoicing of the People of God.

I looked, and there high up in the heavens, above the smoke and poisonous gases on the surface of the earth, above the noise and din of battle, I saw a huge mountain. It was made of solid Rock. I knew at once this was the heavenly Mount Zion. The sounds of sprightly music and rejoicing were coming from a cleft in the Rock. It was the Children of God who were singing and dancing and shouting with joy, safe from all the harm that had come upon the fallen world, for they were hidden away in the cleft of the Rock. There, they were shut in, protected, until the storm passed over.

And with that, the Vision ended.

"The sun will be turned into darkness and the moon to blood red before the great and terrible Day of the Lord comes."

— The Book of the Prophet Joel
in the Bible, chapter 2, verse 31

CHAPTER 9

A Sign in the Heavens:
4 Blood Moons

Eastertide, 2013. San Antonio, Texas.

"What in the world!" cried the Reverend John Hagee. He was alone in his office and his desk was covered with star charts, and chronology graphs, and NASA government reports, and maps of the earth, and newspaper clippings.

The church secretary at Cornerstone Ministries in San Antonio heard his excited exclamation and out of curiosity wanted to check in on him.

"Pastor Hagee? Is everything alright?" she said, knocking softly at his shut door.

"Eureka! I've found it! This is the key to predicting future events! It's been there all the time, but no one has seen it until the 21st Century. The secret is the Blood Moon tetrads. They are harbingers!

"I need to put this on my weekly television program and let people know of it at once!"

Hearing the commotion, an Associate Pastor came down the hall and asked, "What's going on? What did you find Brother John?"

"Look! Look here... the first tetrad of Blood

Moons occurring on the High Holidays of the Hebrew Calendar (as far as American history is concerned) began in 1493, right after Columbus discovered America. That one event changed the course of world history. It was pretty significant, wouldn't you say?"

"What is a Blood Moon?" asked the Secretary.

"What is a tetrad?" asked the Associate Pastor.

"Okay. Okay. Let's start from the beginning," said Rev. Hagee.

"You know the Bible says that as we near the End Times before the Second Coming of Christ there will be "Signs in the heavens," and the moon would be seen as blood red, and all that, right? Okay. Now, a solar eclipse is when the sun ceases to give light and turns black (except for its corona), because the moon blocks it, as seen from earth. And a normal partial lunar eclipse is when part of the crescent moon ceases to shine, because the earth's shadow blocks sunlight from it. Well, a 'Blood Moon' is a much more rare telluric eclipse, a syzygy in which the earth casts a Rayleigh scattering of sunlight, a reddish shadow, across the entire Full Moon."

"But John," said the Associate Pastor, "Rare or not, those kind of eclipses still happen regularly, every so many years. It is not really a portent of the End of the World."

"Right," agreed Rev. Hagee. "But a tetrad of four of those Blood Moons, all occurring in a two year period on the Jewish High Holy Days, is extremely rare, usually only happening once every few centuries, or at least decades. And that is what we are dealing with here. That could qualify at least as 'a Sign of the Times'.

"See, look on this chart here. It occurs first in American history right after Columbus discovered the New World in 1492."

"But what does that have to do with Jews?" the other asked.

"It was a 'Sign in the heavens' of the horrifying bloodbath that was being waged against the Jewish People during the Spanish Inquisition right at that time. Christopher Columbus, who wrote a *Book of Prophecies*, also made it clear that America could be, should be, and would be, an escape and a new homeland for the persecuted Jews of Europe. That is why Jewish bankers financed his voyages."

"I thought King Ferdinand and Queen Isabella did that," the Secretary said.

"Only partially," Pastor Hagee answered. "His main supporters were Rabbi Isaac Abravanel, Luis de SantAngel, and Gabriel Sanchez, and they raised a lot of their money from synagogues and wealthy Jewish businessmen around Europe.

"The Founder of America's purpose for sailing, in his own words, was that the New World should not only serve as a safe haven for persecuted Jews, a forerunner for a new nation of Israel, but also be an international Christian lighthouse, a 'City set upon a Hill,' to spread the Gospel of Jesus Christ to the whole world."

The others nodded.

Pastor Hagee continued, "Then, the second time the Blood Moon Tetrad occurred on the High Holidays of the Hebrew calendar was in 1949, the year following the reestablishment of the State of Israel in the Holy Land, right when all the surrounding Arab armies in the Middle East were attacking the highly outnumbered Israeli Defense Forces, as the giant Islamic nations vowed to finish the job Adolph Hitler had begun, and 'wipe all the Jews off the face of the earth!'

"But God miraculously gave Israel the victory and they won the war.

"Now, the third time the Tetrad occurs is from 1967 to 68 – right in the middle of which the Moslem bully countries in the Middle East again attack the tiny Jewish State, in another attempt to destroy it. The Blood Moons are a portent in the night sky for the whole world to see the evil being done against God's Chosen People.

"But again, the Lord God Almighty will not be thwarted by Man, and again He saves little Israel from the giants in the land. And He does it in just six days, so His People could rest on their Sabbath! The result of the Six Days War was the capture of Jerusalem. It once again becomes the Capital City of the nation of Israel, for the first time in thousands of years. The 'Age of the Gentiles' referred to in Bible Prophecy had now drawn to a close. That is a pretty significant event in history, too, isn't it?

"Here is the point: *That is only the third time in the past 500 years such an alignment of Blood Moons has occurred during the High Holy Days!*

"Each time, this same 'Sign in the heavens' served as a harbinger, a celestial herald, of some momentous event on earth that had just taken place, or was about to in the year following, concerning Israel. And the Blood Moons also always indicate bloodshed from enemies against the Jewish People.

"And now I will tell you what I am so excited about..."

The others in the small group standing in the hall leaned in closer.

"This Blood Moon Tetrad on the Jewish High Holidays will occur only once in the 21st Century. Guess when?"

At this point, the others were all ears.

"The first such red Full Moon will appear next year on Pesach of 2014, and the next on Sukkot."

"What is that?" asked the church secretary.

"That is Hebrew for 'Passover' and the 'Festival of Booths,' answered the Associate Pastor.

Rev. Hagee went on, "This will be repeated the following year. And that means the Tetrad will conclude on the Feast of Sukkot, September 28, 2015.

"Something momentous will probably happen in the 7 year period immediately following that date in the nation of Israel. Something BIG is coming in the Holy Land before 2022 A.D.!"

****

The next week, following Sunday Morning Service, clergy and staff of the Cornerstone Megachurch were in the lobby, greeting visitors as usual. There was a long line of concerned parishioners waiting to talk with the good Reverend, after having heard his sermon on this alarming subject.

An elderly lady approached him with quavering voice, "Brother Hagee, is it true the End of the World is coming at the end of September, 2015?"

"Now, Mrs. Johnson, I never said any such thing. Don't be getting yourself all upset."

"Then is it the Rapture? Is that what is going to happen, Pastor?" the teenage boy next in line chimed in.

"Melvin, I never said that either. Such a speculation would be dubious at best. I merely am bringing to everyone's attention, that if something *doesn't* happen of historic significance in Israel within the seven years following that event, it will be the first time in the history of this country that it *hasn't* happened. But as to what it will be, or when, we do not know: Only God knows."

The crowd of well-wishers standing in line had gathered around in a semi-circle by now, all wanting to hear more.

The celebrated Preacher raised his voice to address them all, "Folks, it could be *anything* that is going to happen. Common Sense suggests it might easily be another Arab invasion of the Holy Land, another War in the Middle East, but I'm not saying I received a prophecy from the Lord on this."

"Why would they do such a thing, Pastor?" one young mother asked.

"Well the Koran teaches Muslims they *must* keep their boot heels on the necks of *all* Jews and Christians. Mohammed called us 'The Children of the Book.' That means, 'The People of the Bible.' In other words, Jews in the Old Testament and Christians in the New Testament. So, they have no choice, because their god Allah commands it of them in one of the surahs of Quran – to keep their feet on the necks of the Children of the Book.

"And if something happens to one of their shrines of Islam under the care of the Israeli Government, then for **some** radical Moslems no other excuse would be necessary. They feel they would be justified in a Terrorist Attack.

"For instance, the Israeli Civil Engineers have been complaining to the Islamic Imams in charge of the Dome of the Rock Mosque in Jerusalem that they need to shore up the foundation of the building because the structure is sitting on a honeycomb of ancient aqueducts, tunnels, caves, and giant empty cisterns and wells, thousands of years old. I have newspaper clippings from the *Jerusalem Post* on it. But the Muslim authorities there, called the Waqf, don't want to spend the money to fix the problem.

So, for instance, if there is a major cave-in and that famous Muslim shrine is damaged, there are radical Islamists in Syria and many of the countries of the Middle East that will not hesitate to claim the Jews did it on purpose, and use that as an excuse to declare war on the I.D.F., because they know Israel wants to rebuild their Temple on the Holy Site, and restore to the Holy of Holies the Ark of the Covenant as soon as it is found.

"We will just have to wait and see what happens, folks. Christians and Jews in the U.S. will simply need to stay alert, and stay in prayer, during that time period – the years immediately following the last Blood Moon. Just watch and pray."

"Blow a trumpet in Zion! Sound the alarm on my Holy Mountain! Let all the inhabitants of the land tremble; for the Day of the Lord cometh. Behold, it is close at hand."

— Joel 2:1

CHAPTER 10

The Mystery of the Shemitah

Hanukkah, 2012. Wayne, New Jersey.

"HaShem!" cried Rabbi Cahn. He was alone in his office and his desk was covered with Torah scrolls, and fat Talmud books like encyclopedias, and the *Code of Maimonides*, and chronology charts, and maps of the earth, and newspaper clippings.

The Cantor at *Beth Israel Messianic Synagogue* just outside New York City heard his excited exclamation and out of curiosity wanted to check in on him.

"Rabbi? Is everything alright?" he said, knocking softly at his shut door.

"Eureka! I've found it!" cried the Cleric. "This is the key to predicting future events! It's been there all the time, but no one has seen it until now. The secret is the Shemitah and the Jubilees. They are harbingers!

"And all this fits in perfectly with the research of Dr. Gordon Lindsay and the key to prophetic events of the future he discovered in the 17 Year Locust Cycle, and with the research of Rev. Hagee and the Blood Moons. They are all in agreement!

"My G-d, man! Do you know what this means? We are receiving an unprecedented warning for the near future! I have to start lining up guest appearances on the radio talk shows. I've got to get the word out! It may start in just a couple of years.

If my calculations are correct, then there may be a 'first punch' delivered in the months (or perhaps years) after Rosh Hashanah, Yom Kippur, and the Feast of Sukkot with its Hoshana Rabbah, when the 'Judgment of the Gentiles' will be sealed for the New Year: That means at some point in the year (or years) following October 2015... Unless, of course, there occurs some mitigating events that forestall or delay it for a period of time."

"What does it all mean, Rabbi? WHAT is going to happen?" exclaimed the Jewish Cantor.

"Something BIG is coming, that's what! Either the Moslem Terrorists are going to strike America again, or the Arab nations in the Middle East are going to invade Israel, or something of that magnitude. Something earth shaking!

"But whatever it is, it is going to lead to a great Stock Market Crash... Not just in the United States, but around the world! America will go into a Great Recession as bad as the Depression of the 1930s. It may even start in 2018, when the suffering in the USA will be at its worst, unless the Hand of God delays it for a little while – for His own good reasons."

"How do you know all this, Rabbi Cahn? Torah forbids gazing into the Crystal Ball. Have you been reading the Kabbala?"

"It is in the Shemitahs, man! It is all there in the Shemitah years of Israel and corresponding Jubilees!

The Cantor pulled up a chair in front of the clergy office desk. "You must explain all this to me, Rabbi. I want to know more!"

The Reverend Jon Cahn spread out a Hebrew

calendar Time-Line chart with Jewish holidays for various years and centuries marked on it.

"Okay. You will remember how Torah explains that just as the Children of Abraham are to work for six days and rest on the seventh day, the Sabbath, so are we to work the land – the Promised Land – for six years, then let the land rest for the seventh year, the *Shemitah*.

"Now, we all have Free Will. We do not have to obey... neither the laws of men nor the Law of G-d. But then, there will be legal consequences when we don't. You can break the law and run a Red Light if you want to, but then you will have to pay the judge a fine. That is the consequence. The judge does not even care if you are from another country and did not know the law, you still must pay the fine. And in like manner, HaShem has plugged into all of creation, as its Creator, certain unalienable scientific principals and behavioral modifiers. So that His system throughout the universe will continue to run, even after it has been temporarily disrupted by the disobedience of either sinful men or sinful Fallen Angels.

"Now, these principals are found not only throughout Natural Law, but also Supernatural Law as well, since the same Creator created them both. And whether or not you believe in them, or know about them, does not really matter. Belief has nothing to do with it. The same consequences are going to happen no matter what.

"Let me give you an example: Torah Law says not to eat pork. It's bad for you. Now, the goyim, our Gentile Christian friends, are not under the mitzvot of Moses. Both their Religion and ours agree on that. So they don't keep Kosher like we do. And G-d is not mad at them for that. *However,* nevertheless, if they do eat pork – as they are allowed to – it still has the same negative effects on their body. Whether they believe in it or not doesn't really matter. Porcine trichinosis, high fat content, heart-clogging cholesterol, and all the other consequences of eating pig meat are still in effect, and thus shorten their lifespan and make them susceptible to a variety of illnesses and/or medical conditions. And that is modern Medicine saying that, not just Religion!

"Okay then, in like manner, there are certain economic principles that come into play concerning Shemitah Law. Whether they are natural or supernatural in character doesn't really matter. They still have the same consequences. Whether it be at the hand of Jew or Gentile, Believer or Unbeliever, whether people know the law or ignore it, none of that matters. The consequences will still be the same, regardless.

"Now, the Shemitah calls for farm land to cease being tilled and seeded every seventh year – to let Mother Earth have a Sabbath Rest. We don't really know why. Maybe it has to do with replenishing nitrates in the soil, or something.

"But we also didn't know why Torah Law told us to wash our hands before eating until a mere 150 years ago, when Dr. Hook and Dr. Lister peered through the first microscopes and discovered Germ Theory. Before that, we Jews simply cleansed ourselves *by faith,* not knowing the actual reason *why* it was important. But here is the point: For the thousands of years before the discovery of bacteria, and understanding its effects, *the consequences were the same* for anyone who ate food, or delivered a baby, or anything else, with dirty filthy hands. The Law didn't change depending on whether or not you understood it, or believed in germs or didn't believe, or were Jew or Gentile, etc. The *consequences* were still the same. Got it?"

The Cantor nodded.

"Now, I am not going to go through the whole Old Testament with you right now explaining what happened to ancient Israel each time they refused to keep the Shemitah Law, we don't have time. Let us just say they paid the price. You can read all my notes here on your own. Then, please give them to the Synagogue Secretary and have her type it all up for the publisher."

"What will the title of your new book be?" the other man asked.

"Tell her to call it *The Mystery of the Shemitah*. It is a harbinger, a warning of things to come.

"What is it that is about to come upon the earth, Rabbi?"

"Well, it is mainly a harbinger for Israel, and by extension, the United States, too – since our country has a larger Jewish population than any other nation on earth and our fate is intrinsically connected with Israel's. But it will affect the whole world, since a Wall Street Stock Market Crash, and subsequent U.S. Depression in following years, would inevitably cause the same thing to happen in other global markets.

"You see, Shemitah Law is all about the national economics of a country. The nature of the 7th Year of Sabbath Rest concerns prosperity and productivity of a society, leveling imbalances, and erasing unfair debtor accounts. It causes credit to be unpaid and debt released. When the law is ignored, it ceases or reduces production and industry. It helps cause national economic transformation by wiping financial slates clean and nullifying debt. This puts a great burden on many people, especially the rich, but is also a moment of Golden Opportunity for a few others, especially the poor, who are wise enough to act upon it. But regardless, it will still end one year later on Elul 29 of the Hebrew Calendar, the 'Day of Remission,' in the Gentile month of September.

"All this is especially true, and magnified, when the nation completes 7 Cycles of 7 Years. Every 50th year is called the Jubilee. It is a time of great rejoicing for those enslaved to debt, since it is their opportunity to escape, and get a fresh start in life.

"But to those who reject G-d, or have forgotten His ways, or enact unjust civil laws in opposition to Biblical moral law, it is a fearful and prophetic time proclaiming national judgment! For a society that has grown proud and arrogant, the Year of Jubilee will humble the rich and powerful, dumping them from their opulent and decadent seats of glory. In ancient Israel, this often took the form of some nationwide cataclysmic event: A war, a virulent disease epidemic, a massive earthquake killing many, or the like.

"In America in modern times (which the Founding Fathers thought of as 'the spiritual New Israel'), we have also followed the same pattern. In 1917, the Balfour Declaration created the *physical* new Israel. (Or we should say it was *conceived* then, and *born* 30 years later). The U.S. underwent a financial collapse that year across the whole nation. Interestingly, it was the Year of the Shemitah when it happened. This began on Rosh Hashanah (Sept.) of 1916. Two months later the Stock Market crashed and burned. The Shemitah finished after a year, on Rosh Hashanah (Sept.), 1917. And within 90 days thereafter our National Financial Collapse was over!

"Now watch: In the U.S. Economy, this same formula keeps repeating itself, decade after decade, century after century, without fail! The worst point in our Great Depression was from 1931 to 1932. 86% of our National Economy was destroyed. Interestingly, that was a Shemitah Year.

"Seven years later, 1937 to 38 was known as the 'Recession of the Depression.' The markets again collapsed. 4 million laborers were put out of work. It was again a Shemitah Year, which began on September 6, 1937. The very next day, Wall Street crashed.

"This keeps happening throughout American history! Look at another example: The Crash of 1973. From 1972 to 74 nearly half of the U.S. Stock Market was wiped out due to the Oil Crisis. It likewise happened during a Shemitah Year.

"And again: The Dot Com Crash of 2000 and the 9/11 Crisis in 2001 caused one of the greatest Stock Market 'day crashes' in history. U.S. Markets did not recover from that financial collapse until 2002. This just happened to occur during, you guessed it, a Shemitah Year. It is impossible that all these could be mere coincidences! The chances of that happening are astronomical!

"And it keeps on happening, time after time. Seven years later the Shemitah Sabbath rolls around again, and what happens? The Stock Market Crash of 2007-08, now called the Great Recession took place. It was the worst American financial crisis since the

Depression. More than half of our nation's markets were wiped out. A terrible calamity.

"Seven years later, that brings us to the next Shemitah Year of 2014 to 15. So, what do you think is going to happen when it comes to an end on Sunday Sept. 13, 2015, New Year's Eve on the Hebrew Calendar, and the New York Stock Exchange opens for business the week beginning September 14th, after Rosh Hashanah? Or perhaps, if the Lord tarries, on Sukkot? Or even a week later, on Hoshana Rabbah (circa Monday October 5, 2015) when the fate of the nations is revealed for the upcoming year?

"Or perhaps, **since it is a mitigating Jubilee Year in 2016, the Stock Market Crash skips a cycle, as has happened before, and does not occur in 2015 at all, but waits for another 7 years until the Shemitah Year of 2022, instead?"**

"O my G-d! I have to move all my stocks out of the market before then!" cried the Cantor, eyes wide open. "Or I will be wiped out for disobeying the mitzvah!"

"Well, I can't set exact dates," said Rabbi Cahn. "It might not happen on any set date – there may be a delay in accordance with the Divine Plan. But an International Financial Crash *is* coming... at *some* point within the next few years.

"And, wait, my friend – it gets even better! You are about to see this system go on steroids! Now, hold onto your seat for the coming of *the Jubilees!"*

****

In the back office of Beth Israel Messianic Synagogue in New Jersey, the Cantor's hand holding his cup of coffee was now shaking.

The good Rabbi continued, "The climatic conclusion to all this, then, is simply this:

"The key provisions of the Year of Jubilee are that **the land would return back to its rightful owners, property would be restored, and those who had been enslaved would be set free, and allowed to return home. It is announced by the blowing of the shofar horn.** The Jubilee occurs every 50 years, both in ancient Israel, and now in modern Israel, since the Jewish People have returned to the Holy Land. It was mandated by the Tetragrammaton Himself and inscribed irrevocably in Torah Law. Its provisions *will* be fulfilled, whether humans cooperate with it or not, whether humans *believe* in it or not.

"Now, in 1917, General Edmund Allenby of the British Army (G-d bless his soul) moved his forces into Palestine to face down the combined Islamic armies of the Turkish Empire. The Muslims were put in fear of this believing and praying Christian man of faith because his name sounds like the Arabic word for "Son of G-d." By the hand of the Almighty, and to fulfill His Divine plan, the anti-Semitic and anti-Christian Ottoman Reign of Terror came to an end in the Promised Land. General Allenby marched victoriously into Jerusalem, now in Christian hands for the first time in over 500 years. The King of England issued the *Balfour Declaration* establishing Palestine as a homeland for Jews around the world, and committing the British Government to facilitate this goal.

"Synagogue congregations in every country on earth exploded into elation and joy! It was a year of Jubilee! Shofars sounded the victory around the world. The Holy Land is being returned to its proper owners. From all nations on earth the captives are now symbolically released, and they begin returning to their ancient homeland in the Middle East. The British Empire conquering the Turkish Empire was a huge event, changing world history. Truly a time of jubilation.

"Now, let us move forward into the future 50 years to the next Year of Jubilee. It is now 1967. Backed by the power of the Soviet Union, the towering Arab nations of the Middle East surround the tiny country of Israel and decide to finish off the job Hitler started: The Jewish swine must be swept into the sea and perish! The reason why this goal is so popular in Islam is because the Koran and Hadith teach only Muslims were created by their god, Allah. Christians are descended from monkeys. (The Theory of Evolution was propounded by the Koran centuries before Charles Darwin was even born!) And Jews are a race of sub-humans evolved from pigs. So, the Israelis are actually nothing more than the descendants of unclean animals, and you will be doing Allah a favor if you simply kill them all off.

"But HaShem, the G-d of Israel, had other ideas. The Six Day War ensues. The Israeli Defense Forces, a modern day David, face certain death at the hands of the giant combined Armed Forces of surrounding Arab nations, a modern day Philistine Goliath. And yet, miracle of miracles, little Israel wins. And they do it in just six days, so they could rest on the seventh, their Sabbath!

"On June 7, 1967, a squad of Jewish soldiers breaks through enemy lines and enters the Old City of Jerusalem through the Lion's Gate. An invisible armed contingent of literal angels had cleared the area around the Temple Mount of all opposing forces. The Israeli squad slowly crept forward in the eerie quiet, wondering what had happened to the enemy. They had won without firing a shot!

"Then they came upon the Wailing Wall, the last remnant of our ancient Temple. Without saying a word, they all went up to it and put their hands on the 2,000 year old stone blocks towering above them, praying in the silence. It was the first time since 70 A.D. that armed Israeli soldiers had done that.

"Tears streamed down their faces and they began chanting in unison our ancient Hebrew prayer, 'Blessed art Thou, O Lord our G-d, King of the Universe, Who hath sustained us, Who hath preserved our lives, and Who hath enabled us to reach this day.' They understood what it all meant and grabbed the local Rabbi, Shlomo Goren, who brought the Ram's Horn. Standing at the Wailing Wall he sounded the long, low, wail of the shofar. The Squad Leader radioed I.D.F. Headquarters and reported simply, 'We are standing on the Temple Mount. We have won. History has been made. Jerusalem is ours once again!'

"The news could not be contained. It spread around the globe like wildfire on radio and television. Shofars were blown in every synagogue on earth, announcing the Year of Jubilee! For the first time in over 2,000 years, the City of Jerusalem was again in Jewish hands, and soon to become the capital of

Israel once more! The property was returned to its original owner. The captives were allowed to come home. The provisions of the Jubilee were fulfilled for the Jewish People yet again, as though the Lord was a G-d Who kept His Covenant promises!

"And finally, we move ahead 50 years more to the final Jubilee Year. It will commence on Rosh Hashanah, Jewish New Year, "Holy Cross Day" for the Christians, September 14, 2015, and end on the eve of the same holiday in 2016. What will it portend? What momentous event in Israel will occur after this coming Jubilee Year, in the 7 year period that follows, up until 2022? Could it be the property that will revert back to its original owners will be the sacred Temple Grounds, the *Beit HaMikdash* ? But before the Jewish Temple of Jerusalem—one of the Seven Wonders of the Ancient World—could be rebuilt, it would mean the Islamic Shrine, "the Dome of the Rock," sitting there now would first have to be removed...

"Could that happen by an earthquake? Or the caving-in of all the empty water cisterns below the mosque? Or an errant Palestinian mortar rocket the next time the Muslim Terrorists attack Jerusalem?

"In any event, if that is what happens, and we Jews are finally allowed to begin rebuilding our Temple, it will indeed be a year of jubilation like never before! Synagogues will blow the Ram's Horn in victory around the world!

"And, of course, there is nothing written in stone that such a momentous event need happen directly on a holiday— Rosh Hashanah, Yom Kippur, or Sukkot. The High Holidays merely start the clock ticking. In fact, the Midrash teaches it is actually Hoshana Rabbah, an octave *after* the Festival of Booths, that is the final day when the verdict of the Day of Atonement is finalized. It is considered the 'judgment of the nations' on that day. I would think, then, there should be *some* sign from Heaven coming in the months or years immediately after that, as to what the future will have in store for us."

After a pause, Rabbi Jonathan Cahn said sadly, "But, alas, the codicils of the Jubilee also make it a time of reckoning, and of evening out. If the nation has turned away from G-d, and persists in sin, then sure punishment will follow, and it will be on a national scale. Unfortunately, the United States is in that predicament now. Our society has utterly turned away from Bible morality and faith. With the continuous enacting of grotesque new laws glorifying sin and punishing the Righteous, I am afraid our fate is sealed for this Punishment Cycle.

"And there is something even more ominous about the additional fact that next year in 2015 will begin the **40th Jubilee** Year since the coming of Messiah Yeshua to earth, and the **70th Jubilee** since Moses gave us the Bible and began Torah Law for the Jewish Race.

"If you know anything about Biblical Numerology, you will recognize both 40 and 70 as the end of a generation – numbers of completeness and finality. That may simply mean the Temple will be rebuilt in Jerusalem and the missing Ark of the Covenant (of the Prophet Moses and the High Priest Aaron) will be discovered in its current hiding place and returned to the Holy of Holies; OR, it *could* mean something far more ominous and final...

"In either case, around the world the coming Wall Street—then international—Stock Market Crash could begin at any point after October, 2015, and probably after the Jubilee Year of 2016, **unless mitigating factors hold it off one cycle until 7 years later, in the year 2022.** But since this period is the years immediately following the appearance of the 4 Blood Moons, and Hoshana Rabbah when the 'Judgment of the Nations' will be finalized, *it does not look good for us.*

"If such a thing does occur in the next few years, other national woes would follow. Muslim Terrorist attacks, war in the Middle East, and rampant forest fires and killer storms flooding the West Coast and Southwest States, killing hundreds of Americans would be likely during the 2018 "Punishment Year" timeframe, or shortly thereafter. Other likelihoods are that this country **may** be in a war or resurgent Ebola Outbreak before the end of 2022, as well, killing thousands.

"And if the disaster is instead one of the Super Quakes that hits – either in California, or in the State of Washington, or in New Orleans and Mississippi River Valley – then our nation will REALLY be in trouble! *Millions* will die. It will be horrible! The 17 Year National Punishment Cycle could be quite severe, **unless the new President we elect and our government leaders reverse the evil laws against the Bible they have made, which now persecute Christians.**

"Plus, if America is not repenting of its wicked and decadent lifestyles by 2020, and we don't elect or re-elect a moral Bible Believing President then, who will not be afraid to call the nation to prayer, then there is a high likelihood he or she will be assassinated while in office.

"But if the United States will turn away from this foolishness, and Congress will overturn the sinful Supreme Court decisions making it legal to kill babies, and flaunt sodomy and homosexual marriages openly in public, or making it unlawful to pray in this country by anyone, anywhere, at any time, and instead enact good and moral laws, and Hollywood is made to stop humiliating Christians and preventing religious Revival in the land, and judges stop persecuting Christians and jailing them for refusing to not break the Commandments of the Bible, and those same wicked judges stop tearing down statues of religious leaders or the Ten Commandments from courthouses and university grounds around the country, then all these calamities will also be made to stop and the curse will be lifted!

"The decision of deciding their own fate is in the hands of the American People *right now.*

"For the time is at hand."

"Jesus saith to His Disciples, 'In the Last Days nation shall rise against nation, and kingdom against kingdom. There will be famines, and earthquakes, in many places. But all these are only the Beginning of Sorrows'."

— The Gospel of Matthew
Chapter 24, verses 7-8

CHAPTER 11

California Dreamin'

(From an eye-witness account article first published in the book *Prophecies of the Future* by Jessica Madigan, then reprinted in *Living Water Magazine,* Vol. IX, Number 2, April-May-June Issue, 1969, published in the USA).

Summer, 1937. Hollywood, California.

A teenager, Joseph W. Brandt of Fresno, was riding his horse in the Hollywood Hills of Southern California. It bucked and threw him. He lay on the ground unconscious.

Fortunately, he had a riding partner who saw the accident and rode for help. There were no cell phones in those days. When they returned, Joe was still out cold. It was a bad concussion. They transported him to Queen of Angels Hospital off of nearby Sunset Blvd. in Los Angeles.

The 17 year old lay in a hospital bed recuperating from the brain injury for several days. During that time, he entered an "altered state of consciousness." He began seeing strange visions. A weird dream kept reoccurring night after night, continuing each time where it had left off the night before. Only it wasn't a dream. It was much too vivid and real.

He asked the nurse if there was any kind of medication the hospital was giving him that could cause hallucinations. But there was not. So, Joe realized something very unusual was going on and began making detailed notes on a large pad of paper for the rest of the time he was bedridden.

Several years later, Joe Brandt and his wife Fran were at a Christmas Party at the estate of their good friends, Jessica Madigan and her husband. She was the author of several published books. Joe was neither a writer nor public speaker, but a humble man who did not usually share private things. However, that night he did speak to the group about his unusual vision, which he had shared only with his wife and a few close friends previously.

The author had known him for several years, knew that he was a WWII Army Veteran, born in 1919, and now a successful businessman, and personally knew him to be a mentally, morally, and spiritually stable man. In short, she knew him to be trustworthy, honest, and intelligent. Joe spoke quietly and confidentially about his experience, explaining he only rarely spoke of this subject publicly for fear of being ridiculed.

Afterwards, he produced his personal diary from that time, the very pad of paper from the hospital on which he had hand-written his notes a few years before. He placed it on Madigan's desk.

Joe explained the reasons he felt this was an authentic Vision of the Future, and not just some ramblings of the unconscious mind due to a concussion, was based on several logical factors.

First, as a boy he knew nothing of geology or seismology, which was a new science in 1937, and certainly not taught at Fresno High School from which he had graduated. At that time, Californians did not talk about a coming super earthquake which they now call "The Big One." Himself, along with 99% of all other Americans, had never heard of any details concerning the San Andreas Fault at that time. Yet, he had detailed knowledge of seismological activities that no layman would know anything about back then (*e.g.,* birds and animals fleeing right before an earthquake hits, etc.)

Next, this vision was clearly out of the realm of ordinary night-time dreaming, as it took place in perfect continuity, night after night, for many nights, always picking up exactly where it had left off. This intimates an abnormal, if not supernatural, character to the revelations viewed.

Furthermore, the viewer was projected at least 30 years ahead in time at the beginning, and maybe up to 80 years by the end of the vision, seeing modes of dress for youth not faintly imagined in 1937 by anyone. That also is evidence of a supernatural characteristic of the vision. Half-sized and abnormally shaped cars were seen, such as the VW Bug, but in 1937 such vehicles were unknown in the United States. Only sedans and trucks existed. And a network of super-highways was noted, which was not even envisioned until many years later when General Eisenhower became President in 1953.

The author listened to her friend intently as he explained all this. Eager with anticipation, she snatched the diary up from the desk. And this is what she read...

[Actual words of the published transcript, written in 1937 (with only a few slight editorial emendations for clarification):]

I woke up in the hospital room with a terrific headache. I remember, vaguely, the fall from my horse, Blackie. As I lay there, pictures began to form in my mind – pictures that moved with the speed of lightning at times, as though time were passing. Some of the scenes played like a motion picture, some stood still like a photograph.

Even though it was California, I seemed to be in another world, somehow, as though it were the future. Los Angeles was bigger, much bigger, and buses and odd shaped little cars crowded the city streets such as I had never seen before. It was like watching one of the new movies they call "talkies," only with colour and smell and sound added.

[*Editorial Note:* In 1937 only black and white motion pictures existed.]

I found myself on Hollywood Boulevard, walking through downtown Los Angeles. Oddly, there were a lot of young guys about my age, but with beards. How odd! And some of them were even wearing earrings like women. Very strange indeed! I saw that all the girls wore really short short skirts, such as never before seen in American history, but it was all the style now.

As the teenagers walked, it was rather different and rhythmic. Some of them seemed to slouch along, almost moving in unison like a dance. I wondered if I could talk to them, so I said "Hello." But they evidently couldn't hear me or see me. Then I realized that if they *could* have seen me, I would appear as funny to them as they looked to me. I tried, for a while, that crazy kind of walk. I guess it is something you have to learn. I couldn't do it.

I wondered what year it was. It certainly was not 1937! I saw a newspaper on the corner with a picture of the President on it. It wasn't Mr. Roosevelt. He was a larger heavier man, with big ears. If I was seeing the future, I wondered what year it was. It looked like the date on the paper might be 1969, but I couldn't be sure. My eyes weren't able to focus on the small print.

[*Editorial Note:* All this is amazing detail of the late 1960s. The description would fit either President Nixon or L.B.J. Mini-skirts were popular then, and had never before been seen. Likewise, the style of young men wearing earrings and having long hair and beards. This was all from the Hippie Generation, as was the popular style of synchronized walking/dancing among young people called "Trucking Along," a fad that fortunately quickly faded.]

Someone was coming... Someone in the present time. It was that fat nurse ready to take my temperature, back in the Fresno Hospital where I had been transferred to.

I woke up. What a crazy dream. My headache is worse. It is a wonder I didn't get killed by that stupid horse.

[Next entry, next day. –Ed.]

I've had another crazy dream.

I was back in L.A. Those teenagers, why do they dress like that I wonder? So oddly. I found myself back on Hollywood Boulevard. I was waiting for something to happen. I could tell something BIG was going to happen, and I was going to be there to see it. There was tension in the air. I looked up at the clock tower by the big theatre. It was 10 minutes to 4.

Then I noticed there was quietness all around, a kind of stillness. Something was missing, something that should be there. At first I couldn't figure it out, then I realized: THERE WERE NO BIRDS. I listened, as I walked two blocks north on the boulevard. All along the houses, no birds at all. I wondered what had happened to them. Had they all flown away? Where? And why? Again, I could hear the stillness and silence. It was palpable. I had never experienced anything like it. I listened, but heard no chirping or other sounds of any animals. No dogs barking. No squirrels chattering. I knew something very big was about to happen.

I walked down the street. In the concrete sidewalk in front of a theatre they had engraven the names of movie stars. I recognized a few of them, but most were apparently new actors I had never heard of. *[Grauman's Chinese Theatre 30 years in the future. – Ed.]*

I was getting bored. On one hand I wanted to go back home to Fresno, but on the other I wanted to stay there in Hollywood, even if nobody could see me. Those crazy kids. Why are they dressed like that?

Maybe it is some big Halloween costume party or something. But it doesn't seem like Autumn; more like early Springtime.

There was that sound again. Or rather, that LACK OF SOUND. Stillness, stillness, stillness, all around. It is unnerving. Don't these people realize that the birds have all fled? SOMETHING IS GOING TO HAPPEN. Something is happening now...

It sure did! She woke me up, grinning and smiling, that fat nurse again. "It's time for your milk and meds, Kiddo," she said. Gosh, this "old woman" of 30 was acting like she was the cat's pajamas. Next time maybe she'll bring me some hot chocolate instead.

****

[Next entry, next day:]

Wow! Where have I been? Or rather, where *haven't* I been! It is like I've traveled to the ends of the earth and back. If only my eyes would get a little clearer so I could write all this down. Oh well, nobody would believe me, anyway. It is just too wild!

This is no regular dream. It is too vivid, like I am actually there seeing all these things. And the same dream continues right where it left off the night before. I have never even heard of that happening to anyone before!

This time I traveled back to Los Angeles, to where I had been before on the Boulevard. A sweet young lady walked past me, dragging two little boys (twins, I guess) by each hand. Her skirt was up to her – well, up pretty high – and she had a tired look on her face. I thought for a moment I could ask her about the animals, what had happened to all of them, but then I remembered she couldn't see me.

At first I thought her hair was all frowzy and unkempt, way out all over her head, like she had not brushed it down that morning. But then I noticed it was just some new strange hairstyle of that day, because a lot of the girls looked the same way, having their hair all puffed out. I pitied her because she looked so tired, and like she was sorry about something.

This was right before it happened.

There was a funny smell in the air. I didn't like it. A smell like sulphur, or sulphuric acid... a smell like death. For a minute, I thought I was back in my Chemistry class at school.

When I looked around for the girl, she was gone. I wanted to find her for some reason. It was as if I knew something was going to happen, something terrible, and I wanted to stay with her – to warn her, or help her. But she was gone.

I walked half a block, then saw the clock tower in downtown L.A. again. My eyes seemed glued to that clock. I couldn't move. I just stood there, waiting. It was FIVE MINUTES TO FOUR O'CLOCK ON A SUNNY AFTERNOON. The time seemed important. But I didn't know the date. I thought I would stand there looking at that clock forever waiting for something to happen.

Then, when it came, it was nothing.
It was just nothing! It wasn't nearly as hard as the

earthquake we had a couple years back. The ground shook, but only for an instant. People looked at each other, surprised. Then they just laughed. And I laughed too. So this was what I had been waiting for? This funny little shaking? It was nothing! I was relieved, yet a bit disappointed. Is *that* all I was worried about?

I started back up Hollywood Boulevard, moving my legs like those kids. How do they do it?

I never found out.

Suddenly, it felt as if the ground was no longer solid under me. Like when you are swimming at the seashore in the waves, and a giant deep trough slowly comes by and you go down with it, till your feet nearly touch the sand, then you are raised back up dozens of feet above the seafloor. I knew I was dreaming, and yet it wasn't a dream. It was far too realistic. Plus, if you are dreaming, and you realize you are in a dream, you wake up. But I didn't. I had to stay there – as though I was meant to see what was about to take place.

There came that bad smell again – a sulfurous stench blowing in from the ocean. I sensed danger. I quickly walked up to a 5 & 10 Store, maybe Newberry's, and I saw the terrified look on kids' faces. Two of them were right in front of me, coming my way. One said, "Let's get out of here! We need to head Back East." He seemed scared.

I could feel the sidewalk trembling beneath my feet. An old lady was walking her dog, a cute little white dog, and she stopped and looked around frightened. She grabbed him up in her arms and said, "Let's go, Froo-Froo! Mamma is going to take you home." That poor old lady, hanging onto her dog.

At that point I got scared. Really scared.

Then I remembered the girl I wanted to help. She was probably way down the block by now. So I started to run. I ran and ran, and the ground kept trembling. Everybody looked scared. They looked terrible. One young lady just sat down on the sidewalk all doubled-up. She kept moaning over and over, "Earthquake. It's THE Earthquake, come at last!"

I wondered what the date was. I wish I knew.

Then, when it came, how it came!

It was like nothing in God's world. Like nothing else! The scream of a siren, long and low, sounded throughout the air. I heard in the sky the tremendous screeching sound of Mother Earth herself. It sounded like the terrifying scream of a woman in labor giving birth that I had heard when I was a kid. It was awful!

Then it was as if something – some titanic subterranean monster – was PUSHING UP THE SIDEWALKS for blocks all around. You could feel it happening before you saw it. It was as if the streets and sidewalks couldn't hold anymore. I looked out at the cars. They were honking and swerving, but just kept moving. They didn't seem to know yet exactly what was happening.

Then, a white car, like a baby half-sized one, came sprawling from the inside lane and smashed right against the curb. The lady who was driving just sat there, stunned. She sat there with her eyes staring straight ahead, as if she couldn't move. But I could hear her. She was whimpering like a little girl. When I heard that, I thought of the other girl whom I wanted to help.

I said to myself that it was just a dream and I would wake up now.

But I didn't. I couldn't.

The ground shaking had started again, but this time it was different. It wasn't a jittery trembling as before, but now a long slow giant wave of movement, like a cradle being slowly rocked. I didn't realize at the time this meant something far worse.

I looked at the middle of the boulevard. It seemed to be cracking in half. The blacktop looked as if it were being pushed up by some giant hand underground. It started breaking in two. (That is why that girl's car had gone out of control). THEN A LOUD SOUND BEGAN AGAIN, LIKE I'VE NEVER HEARD BEFORE IN MY LIFE. A tremendous roaring of thunder!

Then hundreds of sounds, all kinds of sounds, from everywhere all around... Alarms going off, children and women, and those crazy guys with long hair and earrings, all screaming and yelling and crying! They were moving in every direction in a general panic, all running helter-skelter this way and that! Water kept oozing up from the ground, either from broken pipes or I didn't know what.

The cries! All the human pain and misery... It was awful!

Then I woke up.
I never want to have a dream like that again.

[Next entry, next night:]

But the dream did come again. (Or the soul-travel,

or whatever it was). And it was worse. It was as if the first time I saw it, last night, was only the beginning: Just a preview. All I could think was that the End of the World had finally come. I really thought it was the end.

I was transported right back there – with all that terrible wailing and suffering of the people in fear and panic – and the vision resumed where it had left off the night before.

I was right at the epicenter of the quake, in the middle of downtown Los Angeles. My eardrums felt as if they were going to burst it was so loud. Noise everywhere! People falling down, some of them badly hurt. Broken glass and pieces of falling buildings, chips of brick, flying through the air with the billowing clouds of dust. One hit me hard on the side of the face, but I didn't seem to feel it. (Because I wasn't in my physical body).

Now I *really* started getting scared and freaking out. I wanted only to wake up – to get away from this place! It had been fun in the beginning, in the first dream, when I kind of knew I was seeing into the future and felt I might witness some catastrophe, or something, and just didn't care. But this was different. This was terrible! The reality of the actual event, with death all around me, was terrifying and heartbreaking.

I saw older folks in cars, trying to flee the city. Most of the young people were in the streets, looking up at the tall buildings. Those old guys were yelling bloody murder, begging for help from people. As if anybody *could* help them! Nobody could help. Nobody.

It was then that I felt myself lifted up into the air.

I thought maybe I had died. I didn't know. But I hovered up till I was floating over the city. All of downtown L.A. began tilting slightly toward the Pacific Ocean – like tilting a picnic table. Many of the buildings were still holding, though, better than I would have thought. As the quake continued, longer than any before ever recorded, the best of the buildings held.

People saw they were holding, so they tried to cling to them or get inside. But I did not think that was wise. Nevertheless, everything else was breaking up all around them, yet the best of the big buildings kept holding. Still holding. The giant wave-like rolling of the ground continued.

I was up over them now, looking straight down. I started to root for those protective edifices that had been built so strongly. "Hold that line, boys!" I shouted to them. They were saving the city. If the buildings held, those good buildings of the future along the boulevard, maybe the girl – the girl with the two little kids – maybe she could get inside for safety.

Most earthquakes only last a few seconds, yet can do great damage in that short time. Only rarely does one make it to a minute, and the damage can be widespread and devastating. But this Big One, this giant quake, went on for over three minutes! And those three or four minutes seemed like forever.

Everybody was scrambling trying to get inside, because outside debris and thick dust clouds were flying through the air. Those good buildings were going to hold, I hoped. But water was coming up everywhere from underground. It was not just from broken water mains. I could see it from my vantage point hovering over the city, and could tell this was a very bad sign. A dark omen indeed.

I kept hoping those well-built stores and apartment complexes and office buildings of the future could stay standing during this awful shaking, even with water gushing up out of the ground everywhere. But they couldn't.

I had never before in my life imagined what it would be like for a building to "die." It turns out, a building dies just like a person does. It gets weaker and starts to sway, until it finally gives way and falls to the ground like an old man. Some of the bigger ones did just that. They began to crumble, like an elderly person with palsy, who just couldn't take it anymore. They crumbled right down to nothing but a pile of rubble on the street, sending up clouds of dust all around.

The smaller storefronts and edifices creaked and "screamed" like mad when they collapsed – over and above the roar of the people. It was as if they were mad about dying. But buildings do die. I couldn't look anymore at the suffering of all those thousands of people that packed downtown Los Angeles while this was going on.

I wanted to get up higher, away from it all. I kept willing myself to go higher and higher into the air.

Finally, I floated up into the sky to a point I seemed to be out of the worst of it. I could no longer hear their horrifying cries for help. But I could still see way below me what was going on.

I seemed to have risen higher than the San

Bernardino Mountains, because I could see Big Bear Lake below me. The funny thing was, with the eyes of my soul, or spirit, or whatever, I was able to see everywhere, so I knew what was happening even far off.

The earth again started to tremble. I could see it even from up so high in the sky. This time it lasted maybe only twelve seconds, and it was not nearly as powerful. Just an aftershock. But you wouldn't believe anything so minor could cause so much damage. All up and down the Pacific Coast, already weakened structures finally gave way and collapsed.

I saw the streets of Los Angeles County and the whole Valley basin, everything between San Bernardino and the Hollywood Hills. It was all tilting slightly west, toward the ocean: Houses, stores, everything that was left standing. I could see huge highways with up to a dozen lanes, like nothing that exists in my day, still loaded with cars and trucks that had all come to a stop together in one place, on like five lanes heading in the same direction, if such a thing were possible. All those cars started sliding sideways, in the same way.

Now the ocean was beginning to come inland wherever it could, moving like a huge snake across the land. I wondered how far the water would be able to go, how long these gigantic new seawater rivers would get, before they ran into the mountains and were stopped. I saw the time. It was 4:29 p.m. All this had taken place, this massive destruction inundating Southern California, in only about a half an hour!

I was glad I couldn't hear the crying or terrified screaming anymore. But I could still see everything. I saw it all.

Then, though it was like I was looking at a huge map of the world, I was still able to somehow see what was happening down on the ground among the people. Far up north, San Francisco was feeling it, but was not as bad off as L.A. However, it was not just the San Andreas Fault that was rocking San Francisco, as it did in the Valley. That only gave the Bay Area a warning shaking. But when it set off the Garlock Faultline, a few minutes later, that is what did Frisco in. Something deep underground snapped in the earth, and moments later the Hayward Seismic Zone utterly collapsed. I could see the entire Sierra Nevada Mountain range heaving back and forth, making the roaring sound of a thousand thunderstorms for hundreds of miles around in every direction.

I knew what was going to happen to San Francisco. Everyone did.

Once the Garlock/Hayward Quake hit, it was all over. The whole city was basically turned upside down in a matter of seconds. It went quickly, because of the twisting of the earth, I guess. It seemed much faster than what happened in Hollywood, and apparently resulted in total destruction. Thousands upon thousands of people were instantly killed. San Francisco, and everything it stood for, suddenly was no more.

But then, I wasn't exactly there to see it up close, so I didn't get the details. It happened a long way off.

I could take no more of this. The catastrophe was too much for me. Hundreds of thousands of humans dying all at once all around me was more than I could handle. I shut my eyes for a long time, I guess maybe ten minutes, and could no longer watch. I was overwhelmed, so just hung there motionless high up in the air, not willing to see or hear anything more...

****

After resting awhile, I opened my eyes again and saw that the Garlock Fault movement had traveled east and set off Death Valley, which traveled all throughout the southland this side of the Rocky Mountains. Nevada and Arizona were strongly shaken, everything from Reno to Las Vegas to the Grand Canyon. That titanic fissure in the ground itself was pushed, one wall of the canyon toward the other, for hundreds of meters, trying to make that great gap in the earth close in on itself. Boulder Dam was likewise being pushed up from underneath by a tremendous force, and was in danger of bursting.

I looked way down south to Baja California, where the quake had done damage, and to Mexico too. Incredibly, it looked like some volcano down there had started erupting.

[*Editorial Note:* This sounds completely normal, even expected, today in 2014. But in 1937 when this dream occurred, THERE HAD BEEN NO VOLCANIC ACTIVITY IN MEXICO in modern times! (Only a couple of incidents recorded in the history books from previous centuries). The famous Paricutin Volcano growing up in the poor Mexican farmer's cornfield outside of Mexico City did not occur until 1943, six years after Joseph Brandt received this vision of the future!

Now, of course, volcanic eruptions are common all around that country, and would even be expected if a large quake were to hit Baja California. But in Brandt's day it was unheard of, and further evidence of a supernatural characteristic to this unusual and bizarre "dream sequence."]

I saw on this global "map," as it were, all of South America, especially Colombia. Venezuela seemed to be having some king of volcanic activity occurring there, as well. Another volcano was erupting and violently shaking that country.

Way off in the distance, I could see Japan. It was resting on a Pacific Basin faultline, too. But it was not easy to see, because it was so far away. (I was still hovering above Big Bear Mountain at that point). But I did see that some of the Japanese islands were beginning to sink into the sea. I couldn't tell what time it was, and the people looked like miniature dolls, they were so far off. I could not hear their screaming or commotion, thank God, but was able to perceive they all had surprised and fearful looks on their faces.

I looked for the Hawaiian Islands. I could barely see in the distance the huge tidal waves coming in there. The people on the streets were all wet, and very scared. But I didn't see crowds of people being swept into the ocean. They had been able to run inland to high ground because they had advance warning.

It seemed as though I were able to travel way around to the other side of the globe. More flooding in places like Constantinople, built right on the Bosporus Straits. The Black Sea was rising. But the Suez Canal, for some reason, saw an all-time Low Tide, almost like it was trying to temporarily dry up. The Island of Sicily in Italy did not fare well. Mount Etna, the extinct volcano, was no longer extinct. It started trembling and smoking.

England was undergoing great flooding from rising sea-levels, but no actual Tidal Waves. Water, water everywhere! But at least no one was being swept out to sea. People were frightened and crying. Some places they fell in the streets on their knees and started to pray for the world. I didn't know the British could be so emotional! Ireland, Scotland – all kinds of churches were crowded, night and day it seemed. People were carrying candles and everybody was crying for California, though most of them didn't even know anybody there. Nevertheless, they were weeping as if they were blood kin. Like one family. Like it happened to them.

Now, New York was coming into view. It was still there, nothing had happened to it, though the sea-level was way up. Here, things were different. The New Yorkers were panicking, running in the streets and yelling, "It's the End of World!" Teenagers ran into restaurants and ate everything in sight. I saw a shoe store with all the shoes gone in about five minutes. On Fifth Avenue everybody was stampeding. Some radio was blasting from a loud-speaker that in a few minutes the power might be shut off, and they should control themselves.

But they didn't.

Five girls were running like mad toward the

Y.W.C.A. for cover, scared to death. I saw an old lady with empty garbage cans, filling them with drinking water in fear. Everybody was terrified. BUT NO NATURAL DISASTER WAS HAPPENING IN NEW YORK. Some of the people looked dazed and just staggered about. The streets were filled with loud-speakers everywhere, giving instructions to the public. It wasn't daylight, it was night, yet New York City was somehow lighted up like day.

The next morning, everything was still topsy-turvy in NYC. Loud-speakers again were telling the news about fuel storage tanks being broken into, causing a shortage of gas and oil. People seemed to be looting stores and markets everywhere.

I moved on across the country, hovering over the Midwest: Missouri, Minnesota, the Dakotas, and looked out over Cascadia: Canada, Washington, and Oregon. In the Heartland, east of the Rockies, I saw a lot of places that seemed safe, and people were not living in fear. Especially the rural areas, in the Farm Belt. Here everything was secure, almost as if nothing had happened.

Many, many refugees from the cities were headed for these isolated places of safety in the Midwest, some in cars (that still had fuel), some trying to make it on foot, hitch-hiking along the way. I heard on one of the news reports, or somehow I knew, that somewhere in the Atlantic Ocean land had come up, risen from the seafloor. Not just a little island, but a lot of land.

I was getting awfully tired. I grew more and more weary. I wanted to wake up. I wanted to go back to the girl—the girl with the frowsy hair—to know where she was, and if she was safe, her and those two kids...

I found myself drifting away from above Big Bear and the San Gabriel Mountains, back toward L.A. I was perched in the air over a devastated Hollywood, flattened to the ground. I was just there, floating, which seemed perfectly natural in my "dream." The clock tower still read 4:29, frozen in place.

I could hear now, from someplace, a radio station blasting out – telling people not to panic. But they were dying in the streets. I could see something like little moving-picture "stations," or boxes, everywhere – some even right along Hollywood Blvd. These kept broadcasting in real-time, not like a movie, even with all the shaking going on. One fellow talking from this little "picture station" was a short guy, who should have been scared to death. But he wasn't. He himself was actually somewhere out of danger. He kept reading instructions to the public in a loud voice. He said something about helicopters or planes would be flying overhead to bring help. But I knew they couldn't, because things were happening in the atmosphere that would not let them fly.

[*Editorial Note:* This is simply amazing, and another clear sign this was indeed a supernatural vision of the future, not just an unusual dream. Brandt was seeing TV screens in store and house windows all around the city broadcasting live news of the disaster.

Though Philo Farnsworth had technically invented the television in his laboratory some 8 years before this vision took place, almost no one knew of it. Farnsworth did not start manufacturing a commercial television set until 1938, a year **after** this vision takes place! And RCA did not start selling them in the USA until the 1940s, several years later.

Even then, Americans did not begin having in-home TVs until a decade after that. There is **no way** Joseph Brandt could have foreseen the advent of public television and video screens all around the city broadcasting live news, like we have now, while showing a broadcaster at a safe distance far away not involved in the natural disaster he was reporting on!]

The Brandt Narrative continues:

These "picture-boxes" were now showing scenes from all around the doomsday catastrophe. Tidal Waves were rushing inland. Such waves! Nightmare waves! Then I saw again the Grand Canyon's great walls were slowly being pushed together, and giant Boulder Dam was cracking and starting to break apart. It was still daylight.

Then, all the radio stations went off the air at the same time. Boulder Dam had finally burst. There was a complete news "black out" from the West Coast. I wondered how everybody else would know what was happening, people Back East.

That is when I saw several heroic Ham Radio Operators go into action. I saw them in the oddest places, right there with the suffering people, but self-broadcasting from small facilities that had not been damaged; like one little guy with thick glasses. They kept sounding the alarm. One was repeating, "This is California. We are going into the sea! This is

California. Ocean water is coming in. Get to high places! Flee to the mountains. All States in the West take warning! This is California, we are going into the... We are going into the..."

I thought he was going to say "sea," but he didn't. I could see him. He was far inland, yet a monstrous flow of saltwater had snaked in from Long Beach and all up and down the coast, flooding the Valley. His hand was still clinging to the table his radio was on. He was trying to get up, to keep his head above the rapidly rising water, so that he could one more time sound the alarm before he drowned.

I kept hearing his voice, over and over, for what seemed like hours – his final words ringing in my head.

Then I woke up.

****

It did not seem as if I had been dreaming during normal sleep. I was exhausted, not rested. I have never been so tired in my life. For a minute or two I even thought the tragic events had already happened.

I lay there wondering about two things: I did not see what had happened to Fresno, my home town, and I hadn't found out what happened to that girl. The girl with the frowsy hair. I wonder why I care so much about her?

I've been thinking about it all morning.

I'm being discharged from the hospital tomorrow

and going home. "It was just a dream; nothing more," I keep telling myself. No young men in the future are going to be walking along Hollywood Boulevard wearing earrings and beards. Preposterous! Nothing like that is ever going to happen in real life.

And yet, that girl seemed so real to me – the young lady with those two little kids. I wish there was some way I could tell her, (though she probably isn't even born yet), but somehow warn her, that she needs to move away from California when she has her twins. And she can't even be back there visiting in L.A. when that day comes!

She was so real. I really do care about her.

The other thing that will always haunt me, for the rest of my life, is those heroic ham radio operators – hanging on like that after the disaster and trying to warn everyone, to get help from other states, pleading over and over, saying the same thing: "This is California. The ocean is coming inland! Run for the hills! Get to the safety of the mountains. Nevada, Colorado, Arizona, Utah, come in. This is California. We are going into the sea!"

I will hear those voices in the back of my mind all the days of my life.

THE END

"Thus saith the Lord: 'Count off seven Sabbath Years— seven times seven years—so that the seventh Sabbath Year equals 49 years. Then have the shofar trumpet sounded everywhere on Yom Kippur, the Day of Atonement. Sound the Ram's Horn far and wide, throughout all land. Consecrate the 50th Year and make it holy. Proclaim liberty to those enslaved to debt. It shall be a Year of Jubilee for you! You should return home – to your family and your property...

'Fear God, for I AM thy Lord. Follow My decrees and be careful to obey My laws, and you will live safely in your homes. And the land will yield its fruit, and you will eat your fill, and live there in security'."

— Leviticus 25:8-19

Dénouement

The Year of Jubilee

The Eve of Pentecost, 2015. Rome, Italy.

Sexton Timothy scuttled quickly up the Vatican steps leading into the peaceful candlelight of Saint Peter's Basilica. He waited outside the door of the Private Papal Chapel patiently, missive in hand. Vespers Service concluded and a few Roman Catholic Prelates and high-ranking Clergy slowly filtered out. Near the end of the line an elderly Priest recognized him and said, "Yes, my son?"

"For His Holiness," the sexton answered, handing the Monsignor a sealed envelope, then quickly disappearing into the evening. The old man read the contents and immediately turned back into the Chapel. He approached Bishop John, just leaving, an important Provincial Superior of the Salesian Religious Order, handing him the open missive for his perusal.

"The report you wanted from the Vatican Secret Archives. We must talk to the Pope about it at once... This very night, Your Excellency, before he gives his Pentecost Sunday address to the world tomorrow morning."

The Prelate shared his sense of urgency and quickly approached Pope Francis, who was just leaving the Chapel by the back door into his Private Chambers. Bishop John whispered something to him and the Pope invited him in, then called to the Swiss Guard on duty outside his door, "Summon Cardinal Martin at once."

A few moments later, Sexton Timothy, the Papal Aide, accompanied by a man in a purple-trimmed cassock, stood in front of the still open door to the Pope's Private Quarters. "Tell His Holiness that Archbishop Martin left for the airport to fly back to Ireland a few hours ago, but I have his Coadjutor here from St. Patrick's Cathedral."

"Bring him in!" was the answer. And the door was quickly shut.

Behind closed doors, the confidential conclave spoke in quiet voices in the Vigil twilight. "Your Holiness, please excuse the lateness of the hour, but you said you wanted to know as soon as the information arrived from the Vatican Secret Archives concerning what you were worried about."

"Go on..." said Pope Francis.

"Since this matter is strictly confidential, may I ask, why did you choose this upcoming year to be a Jubilee, beginning in the Fall of 2015? Our regular Roman Catholic Jubilee Year is not scheduled until 2025. Is it because of the Jewish Jubilee Year, the end of 7 cycles of Shemitah Years, which also ends this Autumn with Rosh Hashanah, 2015? Does this have something to do with the fate of the nation of Israel over the next few years?"

Pope Francis answered slowly and thoughtfully, "I know it is unusual. I can only say the Holy Spirit has guided me and shown me it must be done. It is important for me to call a special, an additional, Extraordinary Year of Jubilee – specifically imploring Divine Mercy this time – for the purpose of repentance and spiritual revival across the land. That is why I just announced it during Lent, the traditional time for prayer and repentance, before the long hot Summer of 2015. It is a message—a warning—for the whole world, not just for Catholics."

A bit alarmed, the others in the private conclave leaned in closer. "What do you mean, Your Holiness?"

"I fear without a mitigating Year of Jubilee, this Fall of 2015 may begin a time of judgment. But we can forestall it. If we don't, events on the international scene may change and turn ugly.

"Financial crisis hit Greece this summer. And if something is not done, it could hit America before the end of the year as well. If we don't stop it, or delay it, the effects would then be felt around the world. Even if we can only put it off for another 7 years, until 2022, it must be done.

"When it happens, Moslem radicals may target Israel soon thereafter, during the Jewish High Holy Days especially, which in turn could collapse markets internationally. If the USA undergoes another Great Depression over the next few years, even a Deep Recession, it will have worldwide consequences. The rest of Earth will suffer, too.

"For Israelis, and for the Jewish Community in America, and possibly in Europe, the coming 'Days of Awe' as they are called, leading up to the Day of Atonement, may prove to be a frightening harbinger.

I do not want to say anything publicly, thus panicking the crowds, but if we do not act now I secretly fear the season following Yom Kippur, 2015, or 2022, may be truly a decisive "day of atonement" for many people. Great wealth will change hands. Fortunes will be wiped out. War may begin in the Middle East. It is truly a time for repentance. People must call upon Divine Mercy and the Sacred Heart of Jesus for souls to be Saved!

"But such a coming Judgement can be held off, for at least awhile, if the Church around the world proclaims a Jubilee of Divine Mercy. That would buy us time, at least until the next Shemitah Year of 2022.

After a moment of silence, one of the Prelates asked, "And the danger to us, and to all Rome, which the Vatican Secret Service warned us about in that Top Secret briefing? What of that?"

"It is true," the Pontiff said quietly. "I do not know how many more years I will live. There are dangers everywhere... Bishop John, you are a Salesian Friar and an expert on your founder. What did Saint John Bosco prophesy about this time period?"

"Your Holiness, we do not know for sure if he was speaking of the present impending crisis or a future one. But when the time comes, the Vision from God he was granted showed that the Pope would have to guide the Church through perilous times...

"Dark Forces of atheists, and Communists, and sodomites, and other antichristians would almost succeed in smashing the great ship of the Catholic Faith. But by holding firm to the Holy Bible, and all the truths it contains, symbolized by the Blessed Virgin Mary standing on the Pillar of Truth and championing the Word of God, on the one hand, plus utilizing the strengthening power of the 7 Sacraments of the Apostles of Jesus Christ and the Prayers of Holy Mother Church which they founded on the other hand, the Successor of Peter would ultimately triumph and succeed in delivering the great ship of the Church into safe harbour.

"However, the City of Rome itself will burn to the ground in a giant cloud of fire and smoke, it would appear from other Divine Visions. That unfortunately does sound like the terrifying scenario we were briefed on recently in which a Muslim terrorist could easily smuggle into Vatican City a small, low-yield atomic bomb (which the military tells us can in fact fit into a small suitcase), and obliterate most of Rome."

"Will the Pope himself be martyred in this catastrophe?" asked Monsignor Santos.

"This we do not know, it is unclear," continued the Prelate, while Pope Francis listened intently. "However, St. John Bosco's prophetic dreams were clear on two Papal deaths, proving them to be of supernatural origin, since they both came true exactly as foreseen.

"First, he foresaw the death of Pope Pius IX in 1878, exactly one year in advance. Then he saw a hundred years into the future the assassination attempt on Pope John Paul the Great, followed by the natural death of that saint years later.

"But the last Pope in Don Bosco's famous vision of the future had a wonderful opportunity. He saw other Christian boats fighting valiantly for the Faith as well, and they came alongside the great Mother Ship captained by the Successor of Peter, lashing their ropes to her, wanting to be escorted and protected by the Mother Ship. This is clearly prophetic foreknowledge that the time would come, and appears to be at the very doorstep now, that the ancient Apostolic Orthodox Churches of the East would come back into full communion with the Pope of Rome, as they once were; and apparently even some of the Protestant denominations, as well."

The Irish Bishop spoke up, "Your Holiness, perhaps my expertise in the Catholic Celtic Prophecies could help here."

"Yes, please go on," the Pontiff motioned.

"My episcopal predecessor in our Primatial See, Saint Malachy O'Morgair, Archbishop of Armaugh and all Ireland, by a *bona fide* Gift of Prophecy of the Holy Spirit, proven to be correct time after time down through the centuries, predicted that you, Holy Father, would indeed be the *last* Bishop of Rome..."

His words fell on the group like a hammer. There was stunned silence. None dare speak.

After a minute of uncomfortable quiet, looking about him he continued slowly, "But there is wiggle-room in that prophecy, Your Excellencies. St. Malachy implied, by referring to Francis I symbolically as "Peter of Rome," that just as Saint Peter the Apostle was the first Bishop of the City of Rome, this second "Peter" will be its last. The city, that is. The Archdiocese of Rome itself, the Bishop of St. John Lateran Cathedral... **But not necessarily the last Successor of St. Peter, or the last leader of the universal Catholic Church ruling as Supreme Pontiff!** *That* is a regal, even imperial, crown the Pope wears *in addition* to wearing the ecclesiastical miter of the Bishop of Rome!

"So, you see, gentlemen, the Papal headquarters for the Curia is *currently* in Rome. But it wasn't always that way. And there is nothing that says it *has* to be in the future. The whole world is your Diocese, Your Holiness! Was not the headquarters of the Catholic Church moved to Avignon, France, for nearly a century, with 7 successive Popes reigning from there, due to the political wrangling's of national leaders of that day?

"And when the Fascist Party of Italy took over the country before World War II and threatened to also take over Vatican City and the Papal States, could not the Pope have found political asylum in some other friendlier country, and continued to rule the international Catholic Church from there, if he had needed to? Would he have ceased being Pope just because the Nazis took over the City of Rome and he resided somewhere else?

"So, what if Islamic terrorists *do* incinerate the City of Rome, razing it to the ground, God forbid? Will that be the end of the Holy Catholic and Apostolic Church around the world? Would not the Pope, the true Successor of St. Peter, be able to reign with his College of Cardinals and his Papal Staff elsewhere?

"This prophecy may simply mean that the time of municipal Rome is over as the center of the world's attention regarding True Religion. If this were to happen right before or after a new Temple in Jerusalem were to be dedicated and put into service, it may simply be a Divine "sign post" along the way for God's Plan for the Ages – a landmark for fulfillment of future Bible prophecies before the Second Coming of Christ... In other words, a shift in the world's attention from Rome to Jerusalem."

All the learned gentlemen in the room sat back, nodding their heads in agreement. No one spoke for several minutes, lost in thought.

Finally, Pope Francis said in summary of the meeting, "My Brothers and fellow shepherds, we do not know when these things shall come to pass. The time may be at hand, or we may have several years left. We only know that *now* is the time for repentance. *Now* is the Day of Salvation! We must get *that* message out to the people – to the whole world.

"This will be a time of unprecedented opportunity, as well. Even if economic hardships are scheduled to begin in 2022, or whenever the Hand of God so ordains, people must understand that the blessing of the Year of Jubilee goes on! *Divine Mercy* will be given all throughout 2016 and thereafter in an unprecedented way! It should forestall the coming Worldwide Economic Collapse and Middle Eastern War for beyond that whole Year of Mercy. And it may be the **last chance** for many people before the truly Bad Times come upon the earth thereafter – their last chance at redemption."

"Your Holiness, should we cancel your travel plans to the USA in September, 2015, due to the danger of what is coming?" the Papal Aide asked.

"No. I must face that danger. I will not cower in the face of evil. I am the first Pope in history from the Americas. I will go back and be with my people in their Hour of Need. The United States will especially be hard hit, whenever the Crash does come, as a specially chosen nation under God.

"The following years may bring them the beginning of disciplines from the hand of the Almighty – whether a Stock Market Crash and the beginning of a Depression begins in 2022, or not. Maybe it will be caused by another Islamic Terrorist Attack on the USA or Israel, instead. I must be there to comfort and encourage my people in advance of such things.

"Perhaps great and terrible firestorms and tornadic storms will torment them at that time, during their Warning Year of 2018, flooding California and the Southwest and Texas and Florida, with so many Hispanic Americans living there: My own people! They will need me to comfort them. And to remind them through all of that period they must cry out for Divine Mercy, before even worse troubles arrive before the end of 2018.

"But this will also be a Year of Jubilee and rejoicing! The Shemitah Year is when debts are wiped out, and property is returned to its original owners. Vast fortunes will change hands. True, many among the foolish and wicked will lose all their wealth, becoming depressed and suicidal. But it is also a time of opportunity for believing True Christians. Those who are wise, and see what is actually happening in the world at the spiritual level, behind the scenes, and begin living holy lives dedicated to the Lord's Service, in many cases they can expect surprise funding for their enterprises from hitherto unknown sources. Sacred Scripture says, *'The wealth of the wicked is saved up for the Righteous.'*

"But beware, let such Believers suddenly prospering take caution! Lest the wiles of the Devil seduce them into worldliness, just as he did the sinners before them, whose wealth they inherited. Let them take for their example good St. Francis of Assisi, the wealthy young man who used his riches as a blessing for the poor, and to build up the Church of the Living God."

Pope Francis suddenly smiled, adding, "But for now, rejoice! Tomorrow is Pentecost Sunday. We will pray for a fresh outpouring of the Holy Spirit. Pray for Renewal! Pray for Revival! My Brother Priests, *that* is the Good News we must share with all Christians around the world as these dark clouds loom on the horizon!"

- FIN -

LEGAL & ETHICAL DISCLAIMER

1. Though the author of this publication, LTC Harlan, did formerly work for the U.S. Government for nearly 40 years in various positions requiring a Security Clearance above Top Secret, including in Strategic Global Intelligence analysis, he is now retired and has been scrupulously careful to make sure THIS BOOK DOES NOT CONTAIN ANY DoD CLASSIFIED INFORMATION. In accordance with Federal Regulations, an inspection copy of the manuscript was turned in prior to publication to the N.S.A. Special Security Office at Fort Meade, Maryland, his last assignment before retirement from the U.S. Army Intelligence & Security Command.

2. Only a variety of Open Source Documentation was used. The only actual "seeing into the future" that was done was by following various socio-political and religious/historical trends to their logical conclusions, just as the professional demographers and statisticians do at the United Nations Dept. of Economic & Social Affairs with their annual *Demographic and Statistical Forecasting Report,* and Alvin Toffler did with his similar published study, *Future Shock.*

3. The author wishes to emphasize that he does NOT personally believe *all* of these prognostications

need necessarily come to pass, or if they do, not necessarily in the time-frame given. These are merely logical projections, like a weather forecast. The future is a liquid medium, and can easily be changed. All people need to do is take bold action. Our political leaders could save our country all sorts of coming hardships if they would just be brave enough to enact Just Laws based on Biblical morality, rather than caving in to hedonistic and atheistic Socialist trends that invite Divine retribution at the national level.

4. I also wish to make clear I am not now, nor have I ever been, nor have I ever claimed to be, some sort of supposed "psychic" or other form of so-called "Supermarket Rag Seer." I do not dabble in the Occult Sciences. I do not believe in Astrology. I do not gaze into crystal balls. Such practices are forbidden in the Bible, so I have never practiced them since becoming a Christian. It is against my Religion. I should not even have to put this in a disclaimer. It is offensive.

5. Nor do I claim to be any sort of "prophet." Being labeled by that title, also, is usually taken as offensive by most Catholics and Orthodox. Though some Protestant Pentecostal denominations use such a title, and many claim to be one, I have always been skeptical of such claims. By Religion, I am a Christian; by Church membership, I am Eastern Orthodox. We do not have such an ecclesiastical office as that of "Prophet" in my Church. So even if I wanted to, I could not be appointed one.

6. Though I have had experiences with the

Charismatic Renewal, and do believe that the Holy Spirit can reveal certain hidden things whenever He wants to, I do not lay claim to such a Divine revelation myself regarding this book or these predictions. None of this material is original with the author. I am merely reporting the results of others' findings. It may not all come to pass. Let us hope it does not.

The material in this book is much like the News Media conducting Voter Exit Polls to predict the winner of an election. If done carefully, they are *usually* correct. But then, they *may* be wrong at times.

MY SINCERE HOPE IS THAT *NONE* OF THE THINGS IN THIS BOOK WILL COME TO PASS.

My sincere fear is that they all will.

T.L. Harlan

ABOUT THE AUTHOR

Lt.Colonel T.L. Harlan is retired from the U.S. Army. His career spanned nearly 40 years, much of that time spent in the Shadow World of Spycraft. He served variously as a DoD Special Agent (Federal Investigator), a CounterIntelligence Officer, a Global Strategic Intelligence analyst, Commanding Officer of a Military Police unit (same as a civilian Chief of Police), an Undercover C.I.D. informant on narcotics investigations, and other such assignments.

LTC Harlan won many medals, ribbons, and awards over his years of service in the U.S. Armed Forces, including the Meritorious Service Medal while Commander of the CounterIntelligence Detachment at Fort Meade, Maryland, whose Agents were instrumental in the capture of 15 foreign insurgents from the Middle East living and plotting in America, four of whom were sent by Al-Qaeda, and one of whom was a lieutenant of Osama bin Laden.

The author also served as editor for the U.S. publication of the frightening book *I Declare War on Amerika, even from the Grave!* by Sheik Osama Bin Laden. He can be reached for public speaking engagements through the publisher:

Patriots' Press, Inc.
1970 N. Leslie Street, Box 553
Pahrump, NV 89060
http://patriotspress.myfreesites.net

Additional copies of this book available from Amazon Books International, Barnes & Noble Bookstores, and other fine retail outlets.

Available in paperback and hardbound.

Also available as Kindle e-Book.

www.ingramcontent.com/pod-product-compliance
Lightning Source LLC
Chambersburg PA
CBHW020038040426
42331CB00030B/14